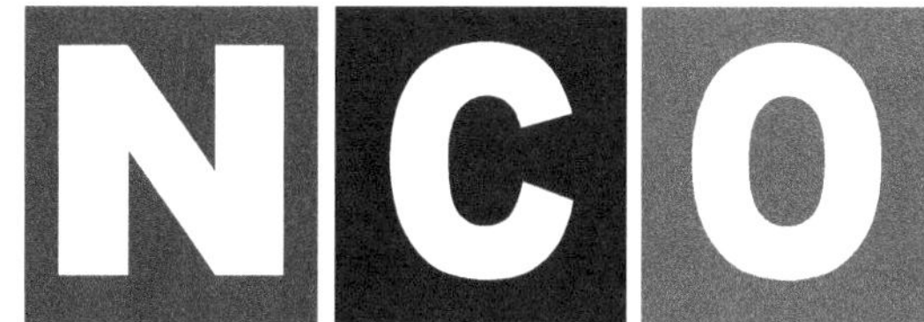

NCO

OLYMPIAD WORKBOOK

NATIONAL CYBER OLYMPIAD

- **01** Learning Objectives
- **02** Multiple Choice Questions
- **03** HOTS (Achievers Section)
- **04** Model Test Paper
- **05** Answer Keys and Solutions
- **06** OMR Answer Sheet

V&S PUBLISHERS

Published by:

V&S PUBLISHERS

F-2/16, Ansari road, Daryaganj, New Delhi-110002
☎ 23240026, 23240027 • *Fax:* 011-23240028
✉ info@vspublishers.com • 🌐 www.vspublishers.com

Online Brandstore: amazon.in/vspublishers

Regional Office : Hyderabad
5-1-707/1, Brij Bhawan (Beside Central Bank of India Lane)
Bank Street, Koti, Hyderabad - 500 095
☎ 040-24737290
✉ vspublishershyd@gmail.com

Follow us on:   

BUY OUR BOOKS FROM: | AMAZON | | FLIPKART |

© Copyright: V&S PUBLISHERS
ISBN 978-81-978176-0-1
New Edition

PUBLISHER'S NOTE

V&S Publishers has carved a significant niche in the publishing industry over the last decade, having successfully published more than 1000 titles across 9 languages spanning over 50 subject categories. Being known for the quality of content, we have built a reputation of excellence and reliability. We have consistently delivered **"Value & Substance"** to our readers, through a wide range of titles across a variety of genres covering school books, fiction and non-fiction that caters to different people from every section of the society.

The **Olympiad Guidebooks for classes 1-10** across all subjects, launched almost a decade ago, under the **GEN X Imprint**, became a go-to-source for the school students in no time, owing to their invaluable and substantive content written in a guidebook pattern,.

Having successfully sold a million copies of the same and in response to demand by both students as well as shopkeepers nationwide; we now present before you our newly launched **Olympiad Workbook Series**, designed for **classes 1-10 across 4 subjects**.

The workbooks are meticulously curated by a team of experienced educators, researchers and subject matter experts, edited by professionals and peer reviewed by teachers. The team has poured its efforts and expertise into creating a crisp and concise workbook which will help and guide the students to the path of success in Olympiad exams. The **MCQs** identified will not only help in scoring top marks in Olympiads but also inculcate a sense of deeper understanding of the subject, by way of solving **HOTS** and referring to complete solutions at the end of the book.

Here we present our new release– **OLYMPIAD WORKBOOK (NCO) CLASS–4** having following features:

- ☞ Based on the latest syllabi
- ☞ MCQs with comprehensive coverage of topics
- ☞ HOTS Questions liberally included
- ☞ A dedicated chapter on logical reasoning
- ☞ Model test paper for thorough practice
- ☞ Sample OMR sheet for real time simulation

We have made sure through our best efforts, that this workbook strictly follows the latest syllabi and patterns of the Olympiad Examination.

As **V&S Publishers** continuously strive to enhance the readability and maintain the credibility of our academic publications, we seek the support of our valuable readers in influencing and enriching the lives of future generations of students.

P.S. While every care has been taken to ensure the correctness of the content, if you come across any error, howsoever minor, do not hesitate to discuss with teachers while pointing that out to us in no uncertain terms.

We wish you all the best for your exams!

DISTINCTIVE FEATURES

01 — Learning Objectives

They list the whole chapter as subtopics, helping the teachers to guide children in a step-by-step manner.

02 — Multiple Choice Questions

MCQs act as an excellent learning aid, helping you to understand and work on your mistakes.

03 — HOTS (Achievers Section)

The High Order Thinking Questions aim to help the student to solve Application-based questions and gain practical understanding of the subject.

04 — Model Test Paper

Model test paper are provided at the end of each book, which help the student to test the knowledge which they have gained after thorough reading of all chapters.

05 — Answer Key

Detailed Answer Key along with explanations aid the pupil to indentify, understand the mistakes they make during the course of Olympiad preparation.

CONTENTS

FUNDAMENTALS OF COMPUTER

LEARNING OBJECTIVES

- ➤ Parts of Computer
- ➤ Hardware
- ➤ Output Devices
- ➤ Software
- ➤ Input Devices
- ➤ Memory

MULTIPLE CHOICE QUESTIONS

1. Identify the given device.

(A) RAM
(B) UPS
(C) Power supply unit
(D) Heater

2. The device shown in the figure is a ______.

(A) Modem
(B) Motherboard
(C) Display card
(D) Sound card

3. Identify this device.

(A) Pin cushion
(B) RAM
(C) CPU
(D) Battery

4. Identify this device.

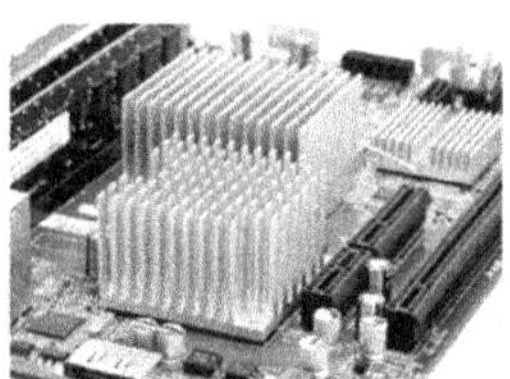

(A) Motherboard
(B) Fan
(C) CPU
(D) Heat Sink Processor Fan

5. Zip disks were launched with the capacity of ______.
(A) 100 MB
(B) 1 GB
(C) 1 TB
(D) 1 MB

6. Identify this device.

(A) RAM
(B) ROM
(C) Hard disk
(D) Floppy disk

7. Floppy disk drives have been superseded by which of the following data storage methods?
   (A) USB flash drives
   (B) External hard disk drives
   (C) Optical disks
   (D) All of these

Directions (8–9): Given below is an image of a computer. Answer the questions that follow:

8. Which of the following input devices are connected with the computer?
   (A) e
   (B) h
   (C) j
   (D) All of these

9. Match the following.

Column-I	Column –II
(i) a	(a) Mouse
(ii) c	(b) Keyboard
(iii) h	(c) Joystick
(iv) e	(d) CPU

   (A) (i)–(d), (ii)–(b), (iii)–(a), (iv)–(c)
   (B) (i)–(d), (ii)–(a), (iii)–(b), (iv)–(c)
   (C) (i)–(d), (ii)–(a), (iii)–(c), (iv)–(b)
   (D) (i)–(d), (ii)–(c), (iii)–(b), (iv)–(a)

10. Which input device can be used to read data from book covers?
    (A) Barcode reader
    (B) Optical Mark Reader
    (C) Scanner
    (D) Keyboard

11. Which type of an input device would be most suitable in a fast food restaurant?
    (A) Barcode reader
    (B) Concept keyboard
    (C) Keyboard
    (D) Mouse

12. The most appropriate input device for collecting environmental data is __________.
    (A) Barcode reader
    (B) Mouse
    (C) Keyboard
    (D) Sensor

13. Which printer would you recommend to your school administrative department to print large quantities of black and white mail merged letters?
    (A) Inkjet
    (B) Laser
    (C) Plotter
    (D) Dot matrix

14. The device shown here is popularly known as MFD. The full form of a MFD is __________.

    (A) Multi-Function Device
    (B) Multi-Feature Device
    (C) Multi-Feature Disk
    (D) Major Function Device

15. Identify this device.

(A) Barcode reader
(B) Plasma monitor
(C) Oscilloscope
(D) Overhead projector

16. Identify this device

(A) USB card
(B) Memory card reader
(C) Pen drive
(D) Portable hard disk

17. Identify this device.

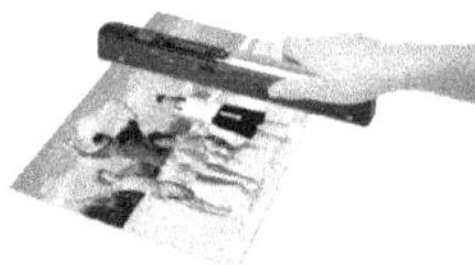

(A) Flatbed scanner
(B) Handheld scanner

(C) Sensor
(D) Web camera

18. Identify this device.

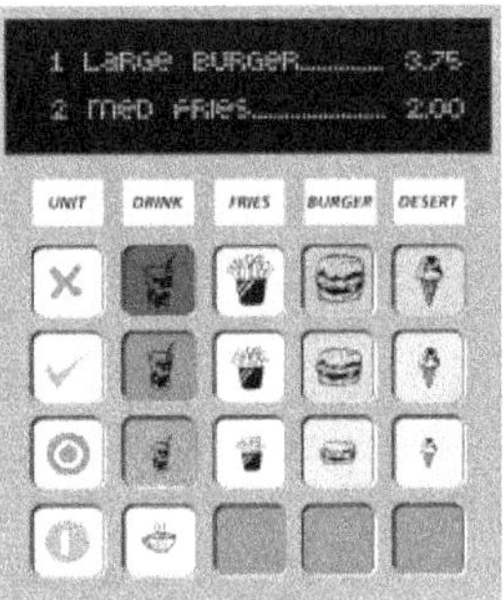

(A) Touchscreen
(B) Scanner
(C) Calculator
(D) Concept keyboard

19. Parts of a computer which you can touch and feel are called _________.
(A) Hardware
(B) Software
(C) Firmware
(D) Utility

20. A tiny piece of silicon which has electric circuits on it is called _________.
(A) Wafer
(B) Chip
(C) Bit
(D) Memory

HOTS (ACHIEVERS SECTION)

21. Computer can perform different types of tasks with the same ease. At one moment, you can use the computer to prepare a letter document and in the next moment you can play music or print a document. What is this characteristic of a computer called?
(A) Accuracy
(B) Diligence
(C) Versatility
(D) Storage capability

22. Which of the following helps the computer to send only the results for output to an output device and not the intermediate results?
(A) ALU   (B) CU
(C) MU   (D) None of these

23. Some common features of a software package are given below. Identify the software.

  ■ It enables users to draw designs.
  ■ It enables users to create graph and charts.
  ■ It enables users to create their overall designs and pictures much faster by allowing them to use not only the graphic objects or images supplied with software, but even those that are stored in files created by some other software or means.

(A) Graphics Package Software
(B) Personal Assistance Software
(C) Spreadsheet Package
(D) Office Package

24. Which of the following statements is incorrect about screen image projector?
(A) It projects information from a computer on to a large screen.
(B) It has become a common presentation equipment today.
(C) It is an input device.
(D) None of these.

25. As you know the monitor is an output device that resembles the TV screen and uses a CRT to display information. The picture on a monitor is made up of tiny coloured dots called _____.
(A) Points
(B) Pictures
(C) Pixels
(D) Spots

──────────Darken Your Choice with HB Pencil──────────

1.	Ⓐ Ⓑ Ⓒ Ⓓ	6.	Ⓐ Ⓑ Ⓒ Ⓓ	11.	Ⓐ Ⓑ Ⓒ Ⓓ	16.	Ⓐ Ⓑ Ⓒ Ⓓ	21.	Ⓐ Ⓑ Ⓒ Ⓓ
2.	Ⓐ Ⓑ Ⓒ Ⓓ	7.	Ⓐ Ⓑ Ⓒ Ⓓ	12.	Ⓐ Ⓑ Ⓒ Ⓓ	17.	Ⓐ Ⓑ Ⓒ Ⓓ	22.	Ⓐ Ⓑ Ⓒ Ⓓ
3.	Ⓐ Ⓑ Ⓒ Ⓓ	8.	Ⓐ Ⓑ Ⓒ Ⓓ	13.	Ⓐ Ⓑ Ⓒ Ⓓ	18.	Ⓐ Ⓑ Ⓒ Ⓓ	23.	Ⓐ Ⓑ Ⓒ Ⓓ
4.	Ⓐ Ⓑ Ⓒ Ⓓ	9.	Ⓐ Ⓑ Ⓒ Ⓓ	14.	Ⓐ Ⓑ Ⓒ Ⓓ	19.	Ⓐ Ⓑ Ⓒ Ⓓ	24.	Ⓐ Ⓑ Ⓒ Ⓓ
5.	Ⓐ Ⓑ Ⓒ Ⓓ	10.	Ⓐ Ⓑ Ⓒ Ⓓ	15.	Ⓐ Ⓑ Ⓒ Ⓓ	20.	Ⓐ Ⓑ Ⓒ Ⓓ	25.	Ⓐ Ⓑ Ⓒ Ⓓ

OLYMPIAD WORKBOOK (NCO) CLASS– 4

EVOLUTION OF COMPUTER

LEARNING OBJECTIVES

➤ Generation of Computers

MULTIPLE CHOICE QUESTIONS

1. A special electronic machine that accepts instructions, processes the information and puts out the information is called _______.
   - (A) System
   - (B) Computer
   - (C) Machine
   - (D) Lock

2. Which computer amongst the following will be the fastest?
   - (A) Processor speed 1 GHz, hard disk 200 GB
   - (B) RAM 4 GB
   - (C) Processor speed 2 GHz, RAM 2 GB
   - (D) Processor speed 600 MHz

3. Speed of a processor is measured in which of the following units?
   - (A) Megabytes or Gigabytes
   - (B) Kilometres per hour
   - (C) Bits or Bytes
   - (D) Megahertz or Gigahertz

4. Which of the following is NOT an example of fourth generation computer?
   - (A) IBM 4341
   - (B) APPLE II
   - (C) IBM360
   - (D) PUP 11

5. Napier's Bones is so named because it was invented by _______.
   - (A) John Napier
   - (B) Blaise Pascal
   - (C) Thomas Napier
   - (D) Thomas Abacus

6. Which of the following determines the power of a computer?
   - (A) Speed of its processor and capacity of ROM
   - (B) Capacity of hard disk
   - (C) Speed of its process and operating system
   - (D) Speed of its processor and capacity of RAM

7. The 'Abacus' is derived from the Greek word _______.
   - (A) Baxa
   - (B) Abax
   - (C) Abac
   - (D) Abacako

8. This device which was made up of movable wheels is called _______.

(A) Abacus
(B) Pascaline
(C) Analytical engine
(D) Difference engine

9. Identify this 19th century machine.

(A) Pascaline
(B) Difference engine
(C) Abacus
(D) MARK-1

10. Which of the following calculating devices was invented by Sir John Napier?

(A)    (B) 

(C)    (D) 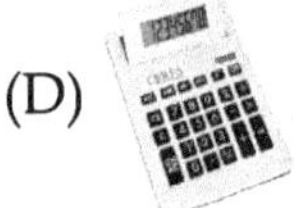

11. The first mechanical calculator invented by Sir Blaise Pascal was known as _______.
(A) Pascaline
(B) Analytical engine
(C) Napier's Bones
(D) Abacus

12. Which of the following was also known as the first general purpose mechanical computer?
(A) Abacus
(B) Analytical engine
(C) Scientific calculator
(D) Mark-1

13. This was the first electronic computer that used the concept of a stored program. It was called the _______.
(A) EDVAC
(B) ENIAC
(C) EDSAC
(D) None of these

14. How is a generation of computers classified?
(A) By the devices used in memory and processor
(B) The accuracy of the computer
(C) The model of the computer
(D) By the speed of the computer

15. MARK-I was the first electro-mechanical computer. It was invented by _______.
(A) Howard H. Aiken
(B) J. Presper Eckert
(C) John Napier
(D) Charles Babbage

16. This was the first electronic general purpose computer conceived and designed by John Mauchly and J. Presper Eckert. It was called the _______.
(A) ENIAC
(B) UNIVAC
(C) EDVAC
(D) EDSAC

17. Which of the following PCs has a touchpad as an input device?

OLYMPIAD WORKBOOK (NCO) CLASS– 4

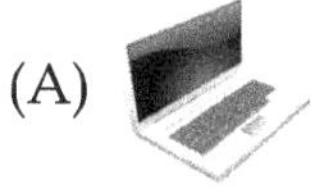
(A)

(B)

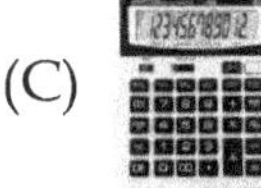
(C)

(D)

18. What is the full form of ENIAC?
    (A) Electronic Neutronic Inventronic Analytical Computer
    (B) Electronic Number Integrating Analysis Computer
    (C) Electron Number Inventory and Computing
    (D) Electronic Numerical Integrator and Computer

19. This image displays the CRAY 1. CRAY 1 is a ______.

(A) Mainframe computer
(B) Supercomputer
(C) Tablet computer
(D) Mini computer

20. ______ and ______ are supercomputers made in India.
    (A) PARAM, VIKRAM
    (B) PARAM, ANURAG
    (C) PARAM, DHARAM
    (D) KALAM, BHABHA

HOTS (ACHIEVERS SECTION)

21. ______ was an improved model of IBM-700 series machines. More than 1000 units were sold for use in business and scientific applications. It was developed in the approximate period of 1953.
    (A) IBM-703
    (B) IBM-650
    (C) IBM-643
    (D) IBM-200

22. Which of the following statements is incorrect about second generation computers?
    (A) They were manufactured using transistors.
    (B) They were more than ten times faster than first generation computers.
    (C) They were less prone to hardware failures than first generation computers.
    (D) In these computers, thousands of individual IC chips had to be assembled manually into electronic circuits.

23. This device which was made up of movable wheels is called ____________.

(A) Abacus
(B) Pascaline
(C) Analytical engine
(D) Difference Engine

24. EDSAC stands for __________.
(A) Electronic Delay Storage Automatic Calculator
(B) Electronic Delay Storage Automatic Computer
(C) Electronic Data Storage Automatic Calculator
(D) Electronic Data Storage Automatic Computer

25. John Mauchly and J. Presper Eckert are the inventors of __________ computer.
(A) UNIAC
(B) ENIAC
(C) EDSAC
(D) Ferranti Mark 1

1.	A B C D	6.	A B C D	11.	A B C D	16.	A B C D	21.	A B C D
2.	A B C D	7.	A B C D	12.	A B C D	17.	A B C D	22.	A B C D
3.	A B C D	8.	A B C D	13.	A B C D	18.	A B C D	23.	A B C D
4.	A B C D	9.	A B C D	14.	A B C D	19.	A B C D	24.	A B C D
5.	A B C D	10.	A B C D	15.	A B C D	20.	A B C D	25.	A B C D

HARDWARE 

3

➤ Different hardware components in a computer

MULTIPLE CHOICE QUESTIONS

1. Physical components of a computer which you can touch and feel are called _______.
   (A) Hardware
   (B) Software
   (C) Firmware
   (D) Utility

2. Hardware can be defined as _______.
   (A) Programs needed to run a computer
   (B) The parts of a computer system that you can touch
   (C) The peripherals and operating system of the computer
   (D) The machines and programs making up a computer system

3. Which of the following statements hold(s) true regarding Peripheral Device?

   Statement 1: These are the devices that connect to and work with the computer to either put information into it or get information out of it.

   Statement 2: Keyboard, mouse, printer and scanner are the examples of peripheral devices.
   (A) Only Statement 1
   (B) Only Statement 2
   (C) Both Statement 1 and Statement 2
   (D) Neither Statement 1 nor Statement 2

4. What does a computer require in order to run a connected peripheral device properly?
   (A) An antivirus program
   (B) A device driver
   (C) A memory upgrade
   (D) A fast processor

5. A tiny piece of silicon which has electric circuits on it is called _______.
   (A) Wafer
   (B) Chip
   (C) Bit
   (D) Memory

6. Select the CORRECT match.

   (A) 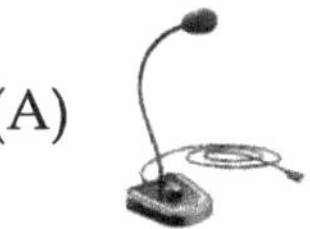 - Output sound from the computer

   (B)  - Input and output device

   (C)  - An output device used to type on computer

   (D)  - Sound output device

7. Which of the following statement(s) is/are CORRECT about the given device?

(i) It is a hardware device that allows information to be stored and retrieved on a computer.

(ii) It is a primary memory of the computer.

(iii) If the computer is turned off, all data contained in it is lost.

(A) Only (i)
(B) Only (i) and (ii)
(C) Only (iii)
(D) (i), (ii) and (iii)

8. Suppose MS-Paint application is active in your computer, then whatever work you have done currently on this application would be stored in ________, but once you turned off the computer that information in this device is lost.

(A) RAM   (B) ROM
(C) Hard disk   (D) All of these

9. Select the CORRECT match.

(A)  - Activity tracker

(B) 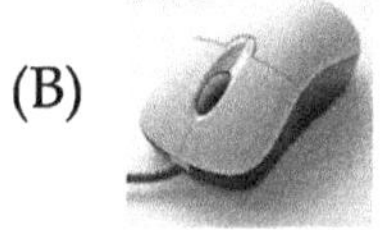 - Scan real world object

(C) 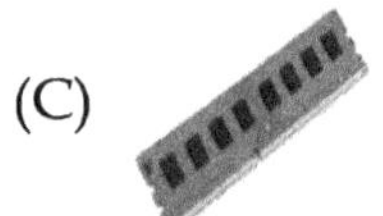 - Swipe debit card

(D)  - Printing letters

10. Identify the following:
- It is a computer's primary memory in which data has been pre-recorded.
- It is extensively used in calculators, washing machines, microwave, computer's peripheral devices.

(A) RAM   (B) ROM
(C) Hard disk   (D) Pen drive

11. In which of the following devices, a ball located on the top is rolled with a finger to move the cursor on the screen?

(A)    (B) 

(C)    (D) None of these

12. Today's computers typically come with this device that contains several billion bytes (GB, TB of storage. It is a computer's secondary memory that provides relatively quick access to large amount of data. Identify it.

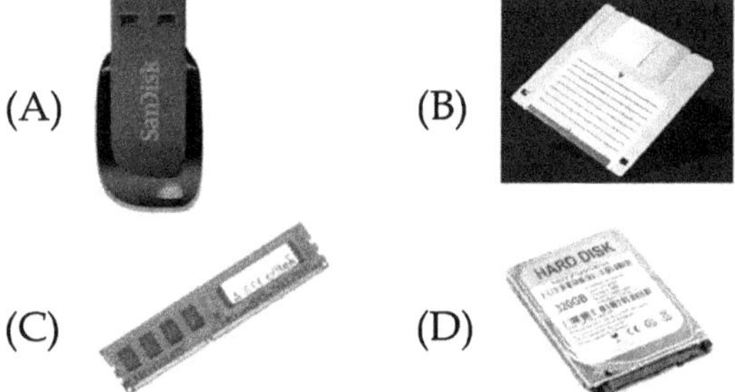

(A)   (B)

(C)   (D)

13. In order to communicate properly with a computer, peripherals require __________.
(A) Cables
(B) Browser
(C) Mouse
(D) Internet

14. Identify the following:

It can be used with touchscreen devices such as tablet, smartphones for inputting data.

(A) 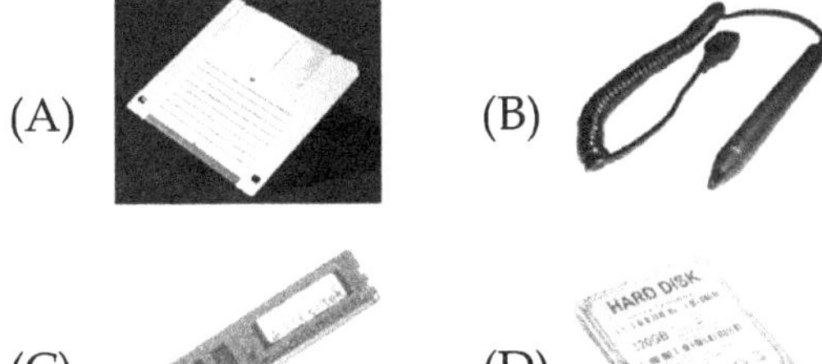
(B)
(C)
(D)

15. Due to some reasons you are not able to hear music in your computer while playing songs. Which of the following devices should be checked?

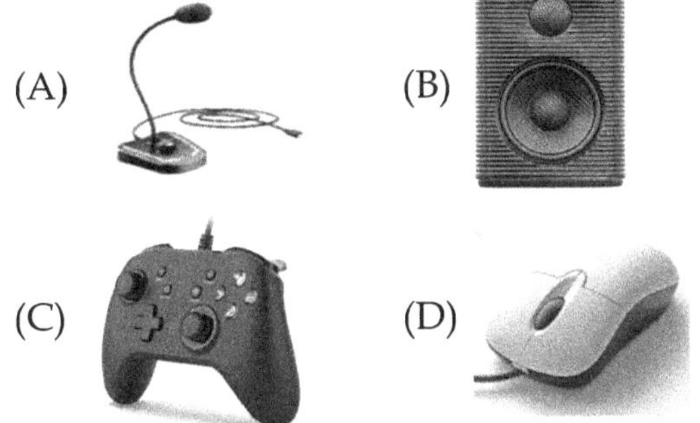

(A)
(B)
(C)
(D)

16. Match the following.

Column-I	Column-II
(a) Optical Mark Reader	(i) Printing Out car designs
(b) Plotter	(ii) Making backup copies of data
(c) Magnetic Stripe Reader	(iii) Reading information from student's exam answer sheets
(d) Touch Screen	(iv) Reading Information from credit cards
(e) Zip Drive	(v) Found in public places and used for providing input

(A) (a) - (iii), (b) - (i), (c) - (iv), (d) - (ii), (e) - (v)

(B) (a) - (iii), (b) - (iv), (c) - (i), (d) - (ii), (e) - (v)

(C) (a) - (iii), (b) - (v), (c) - (ii), (d)- (i), (e) - (iv)

(D) (a) - (iii), (b) - (i), (c) - (iv), (d) - (v), (e) - (ii)

17. Which of the following statements is incorrect about screen image projector?

(A) It projects information from a computer on a large screen.

(B) It has become common presentation equipment today.

(C) It is an input device.

(D) All of these

18. Identify the given device and select the statement which is correct about it.

(i) It is an input device.

(ii) It is cheapest component in a computer

(iii) It contains the device shown here:

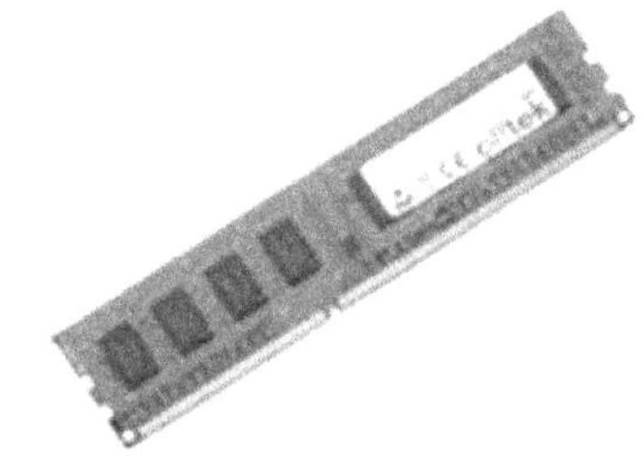

(A) Only (i)

(B) Only (ii)

(C) Only (iii)

(D) All (i), (ii) and (iii)

19. Identify the devices marked as (1) and (2).

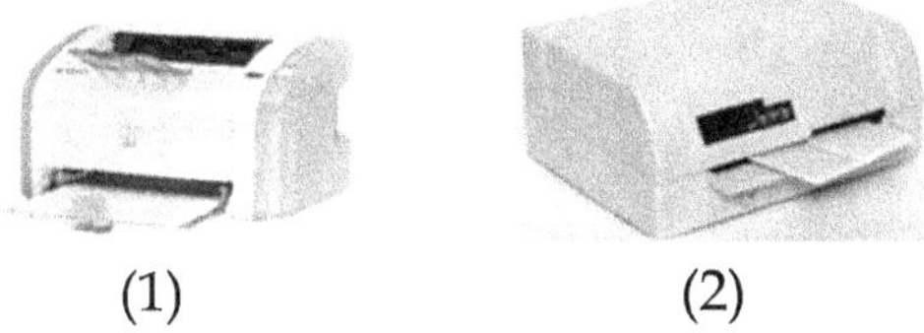

(1)   (2)

(A) (1) - Laser printer, (2) - Dot matrix printer
(B) (1) Dot matrix printer, (2) - Laser printer
(C) Both (1) and (2) are the types of dot matrix printer.
(D) Both (1) and (2) are the types of laser printer.

20. Which of the following hardware devices is used to input voice to such systems?

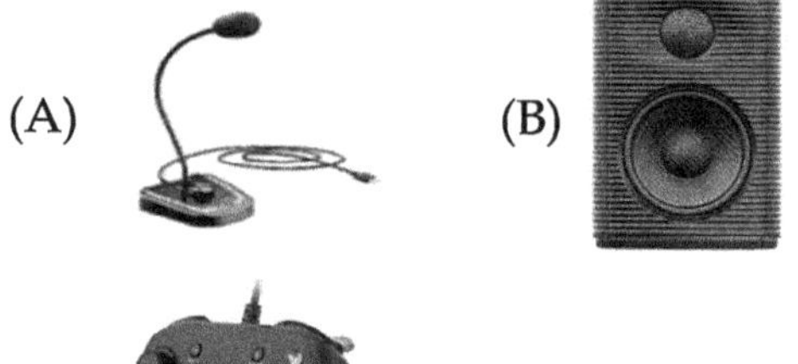

(A)   (B)

(C)   (D) All of these

HOTS (ACHIEVERS SECTION)

21. Which of the following are the predominant manufacturers for desktop and laptop processors?
(A) Intel
(B) AMD (Advanced Micro Devices)
(C) Motorola
(D) Both a and b

22. Which of the following are examples of pointing devices?
(A) Mouse, trackball
(B) joystick, light pen
(C) touch screen
(D) All

23. A joystick is primarily used for which purpose?
(A) controlling sound on the screen
(B) computer gaming
(C) enter text
(D) draw pictures

24. Which device is used in banks for processing cheques to recognize the magnetic encoding numbers printed at the bottom of a cheque?
(A) OCR
(B) MICR
(C) OMR
(D) All of these

25. LCD stands for
(A) Liquid Crystal Display
(B) Light Crystal Display
(C) Liquid Cathode Display
(D) None

Darken Your Choice with HB Pencil

1. Ⓐ Ⓑ Ⓒ Ⓓ	6. Ⓐ Ⓑ Ⓒ Ⓓ	11. Ⓐ Ⓑ Ⓒ Ⓓ	16. Ⓐ Ⓑ Ⓒ Ⓓ	21. Ⓐ Ⓑ Ⓒ Ⓓ
2. Ⓐ Ⓑ Ⓒ Ⓓ	7. Ⓐ Ⓑ Ⓒ Ⓓ	12. Ⓐ Ⓑ Ⓒ Ⓓ	17. Ⓐ Ⓑ Ⓒ Ⓓ	22. Ⓐ Ⓑ Ⓒ Ⓓ
3. Ⓐ Ⓑ Ⓒ Ⓓ	8. Ⓐ Ⓑ Ⓒ Ⓓ	13. Ⓐ Ⓑ Ⓒ Ⓓ	18. Ⓐ Ⓑ Ⓒ Ⓓ	23. Ⓐ Ⓑ Ⓒ Ⓓ
4. Ⓐ Ⓑ Ⓒ Ⓓ	9. Ⓐ Ⓑ Ⓒ Ⓓ	14. Ⓐ Ⓑ Ⓒ Ⓓ	19. Ⓐ Ⓑ Ⓒ Ⓓ	24. Ⓐ Ⓑ Ⓒ Ⓓ
5. Ⓐ Ⓑ Ⓒ Ⓓ	10. Ⓐ Ⓑ Ⓒ Ⓓ	15. Ⓐ Ⓑ Ⓒ Ⓓ	20. Ⓐ Ⓑ Ⓒ Ⓓ	25. Ⓐ Ⓑ Ⓒ Ⓓ

SOFTWARE

4

➤ Basics of computer software
➤ Some common software programs
➤ Types of software

MULTIPLE CHOICE QUESTIONS

1. What is a software?
   (A) A type of computer peripheral
   (B) A computer board
   (C) A set of instructions for your computer
   (D) A cover for the computer

2. When your teacher asks a question in the class, you simply raise your hand if you know the answer. It is your brain that prompts you to raise the hand or you can say, it gives you instructions to react like this. Similarly, a computer gets all the instructions from the ___________ to perform various tasks.
   (A) Faux ware   (B) Software
   (C) Netware   (D) Appware

3. Which of the following is a software?
   (A) Almirah   (B) MS Word
   (C) Monitor   (D) Printer

4. What do application programs do?
   (A) Enable the RAM to load information.
   (B) Enable the user to perform a task.
   (C) Enable the BIOS instructions to load on hard disk.
   (D) Both (A) and (B)

5. What are the two main types of software?

   i.   Application software
   ii. System software
   iii. Language processor software
   (A) (i) and (ii)
   (B) (i) and (iii)
   (C) (ii) and (iii)
   (D) None of these

6. Observe the given software logos and select the statement which is CORRECT about them.

   i. They are operating systems. They are the examples of system software, without which a computer cannot work.
   ii. As a driver is required to run a car, similarly they are needed to operate a computer.
   (A) Only (i)
   (B) Only (ii)
   (C) Both (i) and (ii)
   (D) Neither (i) nor (ii)

7. Identify the following:
   - It is an application program that can run on your desktop computer, laptop or smartphones.
   - It enables you to upload photos and interact with your friends and family.
   (A) Facebook
   (B) Intel
   (C) Infosys
   (D) Wipro

8. Which of the following statements hold(s) true regarding the given software?

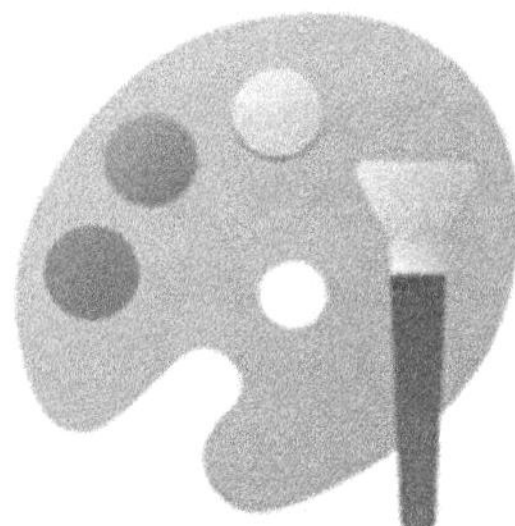

   Statement 1: It is a graphic software that is used to create images.

   Statement 2: It comes under the category of system software.
   (A) Only Statement 1
   (B) Only Statement 2
   (C) Both Statement 1 and Statement 2
   (D) Neither Statement 1 nor Statement 2

9. Utilities are the programs that assist in the smooth functioning of a computer. Some utilities help you to:
   (1) Avoid virus attack.
   (2) Take backup of data.
   (3) Recover data that has been accidentally erased.
   Which of the following is a utility software?
   (A) Twitter
   (B) Antivirus
   (C) Facebook
   (D) Instagram

10. Videos and music on a computer can be played using which of the following software?
    (A) MS Office   (B) Coreldraw
    (C) Media player   (D) Antivirus

11. Which of the following is NOT a software?
    (A) MS Office   (B) Coreldraw
    (C) Intel   (D) Antivirus

12. Which of the following is a file management software in Windows 7?
    (A) Calculator
    (B) Internet Explorer
    (C) Windows Explorer
    (D) MS-Paint

13. Which of the following software is used to play music on Windows?
    (A) Windows Media Player
    (B) Windows Sound Recorder
    (C) Windows Sync Center
    (D) Sticky Notes

14. Which of the following types of software is used in electronic system such as TV remote, washing machines, etc.?
    (A) System   (B) Firmware
    (C) URL   (D) Sync Centre

15. What is file management?
    (A) A person who manages files
    (B) Keeping files and folders organized
    (C) A file cabinet
    (D) A floppy disk

16. Identify the software package by its given features.
    - It enables users to draw designs.
    - It enables users to create graphs and charts.
    - It enables users to create their overall designs and pictures much faster by allowing them to use not only the graphic objects or images supplied with software, but even those that are stored in files created by some other software or means.

OLYMPIAD WORKBOOK (NCO) CLASS— 4

(A) Graphics Package Software
(B) Personal Assistance Software
(C) Spreadsheet Package
(D) Office Package

17. Select the INCORRECT match regarding the software with their descriptions.
    (A) Whatsapp - An application software and an instant messaging service.
    (B) Android - System software and a mobile operating system.
    (C) Norton - Utility program and a file management application.
    (D) Twitter - A social networking app.

18. Logos of some software are given here and below them the type of software they belong to is written. Select which among the following is labelled incorrectly.

 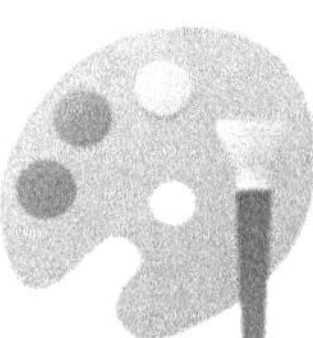 

(i)	(ii)	(iii)
Operating System	Application software	Application software

(A) Only (i)
(B) Only (ii)
(C) Only (iii)
(D) Both (i) and (ii)

19. A word processing software helps to create professional looking documents quickly and efficiently. Now, answer the questions that follow. Which of the following is a word processing software?
    (A) MS Word
    (B) Wordpress
    (C) MS Paint
    (D) Both (A) and (B)

20. A word processing software helps to create professional looking documents quickly and efficiently. Now, answer the questions that follow. These software provide many features to change the text in a desired manner. You can __________.
    (A) Add, delete and rearrange the text
    (B) Beautify the text
    (C) Produce a hardcopy of the document as required
    (D) All of these

HOTS (ACHIEVERS SECTION)

21. __________ are words that a programming language has set aside for its own use ?
    (A) Control words
    (B) Control structures
    (C) Reserved words
    (D) Reserved keys

22. Which of the following software could assist someone who cannot use their hands for computer input ?
    (A) Video conferencing
    (B) Speech recognition
    (C) Audio digitizer
    (D) Synthesizer

23. __________ is the process of finding errors in software code ?
    (A) Hacking   (B) Compiling
    (C) Testing   (D) Debugging

24. A series of instructions that tells a computer what to do and how to do it is called a __________ ?

(A) program

(B) command

(C) user response

(D) processor

25. System software

(A) allows the user to diagnose and troubleshoot the device

(B) is a programming language

(C) is part of a productivity suite

(D) helps the computer manage internal resources

1.	A B C D	6.	A B C D	11.	A B C D	16.	A B C D	21.	A B C D
2.	A B C D	7.	A B C D	12.	A B C D	17.	A B C D	22.	A B C D
3.	A B C D	8.	A B C D	13.	A B C D	18.	A B C D	23.	A B C D
4.	A B C D	9.	A B C D	14.	A B C D	19.	A B C D	24.	A B C D
5.	A B C D	10.	A B C D	15.	A B C D	20.	A B C D	25.	A B C D

OLYMPIAD WORKBOOK (NCO) CLASS – 4

MS PAINT

➤ The Paint Window
➤ The Ribbon
➤ The Tools Menu

MULTIPLE CHOICE QUESTIONS

1. While working with text, you can change the font type and font size using ________.
   (A) Text pop-up   (B) View menu
   (C) Text tab   (D) Design box

2. Which of the following is not a tool in Paint?
   (A) Brush tool   (B) Polish tool
   (C) Fill tool   (D) Color picker

3. This menu is displayed when you _____.

   (A) Click on **B** in the Home Tab of the ribbon
   (B) Select the text tool, and you select an area to enter text
   (C) Want to change the font size
   (D) All of these

4. What is the name of the tool used to fill a shape with colour called?
   (A) Colour tool
   (B) Fill tool
   (C) Fill color tool
   (D) Paint tool

5. The size of the image properties dialog box is not displayed in ________.
   (A) Inches   (B) Pixels
   (C) Dots   (D) Centimeters

6. Which of the following operations on text cannot be done using the Menu shown below?

   (A) Bold   (B) Italic
   (C) Superscript   (D) Strikethrough

7. The image properties dialog box in MS Paint can also be used to set the colors. Which of the following options can be set in MS Paint?
   (A) Black and white, color
   (B) RGB, CMYK
   (C) Grayscale, Color
   (D) None of these

8. In MS Paint, a picture can be skewed ______.
   (A) Only horizontally
   (B) Both horizontally and vertically
   (C) Only vertically
   (D) None of these

9. You can change the height and width of a picture using ______.
   (A) Image → Resize and Skew → Resize
   (B) Image → Resize and Skew → Flip Vertically
   (C) Paint Button → Width, Height
   (D) All of these

10. You can change the height and width of the drawing area using ______.
   (A) Image → Resize and Skew → Rotate 90°
   (B) Image → Resize and Skew → Flip Vertically
   (C) Paint Button → Properties → Width, Height
   (D) All of these

11. Which of the following operations would give an inverted mirror image of the picture?
   (A) Rotate 180°   (B) Flip horizontal
   (C) Flip vertical   (D) Rotate 90°

12. While creating the given image, the designer accidentally saved the image up-side down as shown in Image-I. Which operation should be used to correct the problem and show it in the correct direction as in Image-II?

   Image-I   **Image-II**

   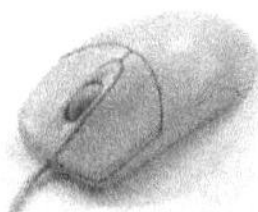   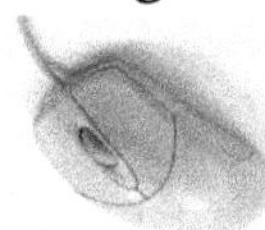

   (A) Rotate right 90°
   (B) Flip vertical
   (C) Skew
   (D) Flip horizontal

13. Which operation might have been performed to get Image-II from Image-I?

   Image-I   **Image-II**

      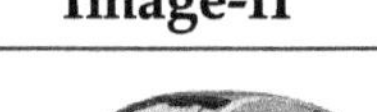

   (A) Stretch
   (B) Skew horizontal
   (C) Skew vertical
   (D) Flip vertical

14. Which of the following options is not a selection shape?
   (A)    (B)
   (C)   (D) 

15. In MS Paint, which of the following options is used to view the drawing as it will look when printed?
   (A) Print preview
   (B) Page set up
   (C) Print selected
   (D) Page layout

16. Match the following.

Column-I	Column-II
(i) Skew	(a) To change the drawing to its mirror image
(ii) Thumbnail	(b) To rotate the drawing through a given angle
(iii) Bitmap	(c) To display the drawing in a small reference window
(iv) Flip	(d) File format to store Paint files

   (A) (i)–(a), (ii)–(c), (iii)–(d), (iv)–(b)
   (B) (i)–(a), (ii)–(d), (iii)–(c), (iv)–(b)
   (C) (i)–(b), (ii)–(d), (iii)–(c), (iv)–(a)
   (D) (i)–(b), (ii)–(c), (iii)–(d), (iv)–(a)

17. To draw a red circle with a blue boundary, you should set ______.
   (A) Color 1 to blue, Color 2 to red and fill style to solid color

(B) Color 2 to blue, Color 1 to red and fill style to solid color

(C) Color 1 to first red and then blue, fill style to solid color

(D) You cannot draw such a circle with MS Paint

18. Match the following.

Column-I	Column-II
(i) No Fill	(a)
(ii) Natural Pencil	(b)
(iii) Solid Fill	(c)
(iv) Crayon	(d)

(A) (i)–(c), (ii)–(d), (iii)–(a), (iv)–(b)
(B) (i)–(c), (ii)–(d), (iii)–(b), (iv)–(a)
(C) (i)–(d), (ii)–(c), (iii)–(b), (iv)–(a)
(D) (i)–(d), (ii)–(c), (iii)–(a), (iv)–(b)

19. To draw a circle with no boundary, what should you do?

(A) Set the shape outline style to No outline
(B) Set the shape outline to solid Color
(C) Use the same Color1 and Color2
(D) None of these

20. Which of the following is not a shape outline style?
(A) Natural pencil
(B) Watercolor
(C) No outline
(D) No fill

HOTS (ACHIEVERS SECTION)

21. How can you add colors in the unfilled box in the colors group of Home tab in MS Paint of Windows?

(A) Click on <Color 1> button → select Custom Colors in Edit Colors in Edit Colors dialog box → click on 'Add to Custom Colors' → click ok.

(B) Click on <Color 2> button box → select Custom Colors in Edit color dialog box → click on 'Add to Custom Colors' → click ok.

(C) Click on <Edit colors> box → select Custom Color in Edit Color dialog box → click on ' Add To Custom Colors' → click ok.

(D) Both (a) and (b)

22. Find the odd one out.

(A)   (B)

(C)   (D)

23. Given below is the information about paint tools. Select the correct statements.
i.   The tool used to make your drawing look bigger is called Magnifier tool.
ii. Fill tool is a tool for writing in the Paint Brush Program.
iii. Text tool is a tool to apply color to a large area of text.
(A) Only i
(B) i and ii
(C) i and iii
(D) ii and iii

24. Fill in the Blanks:
i.   The Paint Brush opens and saves files with a __________ extension.

ii. ____________ is the extension used for PowerPoint files.

iii. Document files use ____________ extension to save a file.

(A) .ppt, .pmb, .doc

(B) .bmp, .ppt, .doc

(C) .pmb, .ppf, .txt

(D) .bmp, .ppt, .txt

25. Read the given statements and select the correct one.

i. Paint brush is a program which is only used for drawing the picture. You cannot colour and edit the pictures.

ii. Stretch will let you change the proportions of the selection, making them narrower, wider, shorter or taller.

iii. Select All command automatically selects the entire image.

(A) i and ii

(B) i and iii

(C) ii and iii

(D) All of these

Darken Your Choice with HB Pencil

1.	A B C D	6.	A B C D	11.	A B C D	16.	A B C D	21.	A B C D
2.	A B C D	7.	A B C D	12.	A B C D	17.	A B C D	22.	A B C D
3.	A B C D	8.	A B C D	13.	A B C D	18.	A B C D	23.	A B C D
4.	A B C D	9.	A B C D	14.	A B C D	19.	A B C D	24.	A B C D
5.	A B C D	10.	A B C D	15.	A B C D	20.	A B C D	25.	A B C D

INTERNET AND ITS USES

LEARNING OBJECTIVES

- ➤ Blog or Web Log
- ➤ Internet
- ➤ Server
- ➤ URL

MULTIPLE CHOICE QUESTIONS

1. The address of a website is known as ________. It is entered in the ______ bar of the browser window.
   - (A) URL, hyperlinks
   - (B) URL, address
   - (C) Hyperlinks, address
   - (D) Address, hyperlinks

2. What can you do using the Internet?
   - (A) Download software
   - (B) Participate in interactive forums
   - (C) Chat with your friends
   - (D) All of these

3. HTTP stands for ______.
   - (A) Hypertext Transfer Protocol
   - (B) Hyphentext Transfer Protocol
   - (C) Hypertext Transfer Provider
   - (D) Hypertransfer Text Protocol

4. The rule followed in the transmission of information on the Internet is called ________.
   - (A) Internet Protocols
   - (B) Internet Police
   - (C) Interpol Police
   - (D) Interpol Protocol

5. What all do you need to connect to the Internet?
   - (A) Internet Service Provider
   - (B) Modem
   - (C) Software
   - (D) All of these

6. Internet Service Providers are the companies that give you access to the ________.
   - (A) Documents
   - (B) Files
   - (C) Internet
   - (D) Node

7. ______ is a piece of hardware that serves in exchanging information between two computers through the cables.
   - (A) Wire
   - (B) Modem
   - (C) Scanner
   - (D) None of these

8. A Client Program (software) that is used to look at various kinds of Internet resources is called a/an ______.
   - (A) Address
   - (B) Provider
   - (C) Browser
   - (D) Protocol

9. Web pages are written using ______.
   (A) Network
   (B) HTML
   (C) URL
   (D) Website

10. Which of the following is not a web browser?
    (A) Chrome
    (B) Mozilla
    (C) Internet explorer
    (D) Windows explorer

11. Which of the following is not an Indian ISP?
    (A) Verizon
    (B) Jio
    (C) Spectranet
    (D) Airtel

12. Who developed the World Wide Web?
    (A) Sir Tim Berners-Lee
    (B) Taub-Schilling
    (C) Dennis Richie
    (D) Ronald Trump

13. How many types of modems are there?
    (A) 6
    (B) 3
    (C) 4
    (D) 5

14. Which of the following is not a search engine?
    (A) Bing
    (B) Yahoo
    (C) Meta Crawler
    (D) Facebook

15. Internet can be used for which of the following?
    (A) Buying and selling old and new goods
    (B) Checking exam results
    (C) Performing banking operations
    (D) All of these

16. The internet runs on a set of protocols called ______.
    (A) FTP
    (B) TCP/IP
    (C) HTTP
    (D) SMTP

17. What is FTP primarily used for?
    (A) Transferring files over the Internet
    (B) Sending secure e-mail messages
    (C) Establishing firewalls within networks
    (D) Routing fiber-optic connections

18. Which of the following is a popular website to view videos of latest songs and movies?
    (A)
    (B)
    (C)
    (D)

19. Internet is used for audio and video calling across geographies. A popular tool for such internet call is ______.
    (A)
    (B)
    (C)
    (D)

20. Which of the following is a popular auction site on the internet?
    (A)
    (B)
    (C)
    (D)

21. Which of the following translates a name like shraddhasingh.com into numbers like 16.01.88.04?

    (A) DNS

    (B) IP address

    (C) E-mail

    (D) Port

22. www.pinki.info, www.sheetal.net, www.shraddha.name are examples of ________.

    (A) Country Domains

    (B) Generic Domains

    (C) Specialized Domains

    (D) Vanity Domains

23. Net 2 phone is a/an __________.

    (A) Internal phone program that allows you to make calls over the internet

    (B) Instant messaging program

    (C) Web editing program

    (D) Tool for participating in newsgroup over telephone

24. Port number for outgoing e-mail is __________ and port number for incoming e-mail is ________.

    (A) 110, 25   (B) 25, 110

    (C) 80, 25   (D) 25, 80

25. What is the term for unsolicited Email?

    (A) Spam   (B) Backbone

    (C) Usenet   (D) News group

Darken Your Choice with HB Pencil

1. Ⓐ Ⓑ Ⓒ Ⓓ	6. Ⓐ Ⓑ Ⓒ Ⓓ	11. Ⓐ Ⓑ Ⓒ Ⓓ	16. Ⓐ Ⓑ Ⓒ Ⓓ	21. Ⓐ Ⓑ Ⓒ Ⓓ
2. Ⓐ Ⓑ Ⓒ Ⓓ	7. Ⓐ Ⓑ Ⓒ Ⓓ	12. Ⓐ Ⓑ Ⓒ Ⓓ	17. Ⓐ Ⓑ Ⓒ Ⓓ	22. Ⓐ Ⓑ Ⓒ Ⓓ
3. Ⓐ Ⓑ Ⓒ Ⓓ	8. Ⓐ Ⓑ Ⓒ Ⓓ	13. Ⓐ Ⓑ Ⓒ Ⓓ	18. Ⓐ Ⓑ Ⓒ Ⓓ	23. Ⓐ Ⓑ Ⓒ Ⓓ
4. Ⓐ Ⓑ Ⓒ Ⓓ	9. Ⓐ Ⓑ Ⓒ Ⓓ	14. Ⓐ Ⓑ Ⓒ Ⓓ	19. Ⓐ Ⓑ Ⓒ Ⓓ	24. Ⓐ Ⓑ Ⓒ Ⓓ
5. Ⓐ Ⓑ Ⓒ Ⓓ	10. Ⓐ Ⓑ Ⓒ Ⓓ	15. Ⓐ Ⓑ Ⓒ Ⓓ	20. Ⓐ Ⓑ Ⓒ Ⓓ	25. Ⓐ Ⓑ Ⓒ Ⓓ

COMPUTER NETWORK

LEARNING OBJECTIVES

➤ Types of Network

➤ Uses of Networks

MULTIPLE CHOICE QUESTIONS

1. This is the center of a computer network.
   (A) File server
   (B) Document
   (C) Control unit
   (D) Software

2. LAN stands for
   (A) Land Area Network
   (B) Local Arial Networking
   (C) Local Area Network
   (D) Load Assessment Network

3. Which is a popular Operating System?
   (A) Unix
   (B) MS-Windows
   (C) Windows NT
   (D) All of these

4. Every computer in a network is called a
   _______.
   (A) Point   (B) System
   (C) Node   (D) None of these

5. WAN stands for _______.
   (A) Wide Area Network
   (B) World Area Network
   (C) World Arial Network
   (D) World Assessment Network

6. When a network of computers within a school are connected with cables, it is called _______.
   (A) LAN
   (B) WAN
   (C) MAN
   (D) None of these

7. A network where computers share data and programs over long distances across the world is called _______.
   (A) LAN
   (B) WAN
   (C) MAN
   (D) None of these

8. _______ converts digital signals to audible analog tones.
   (A) Converter
   (B) Modular
   (C) Transformer
   (D) Modem

9. A group of computers connected together is called a _______.
   (A) Station   (B) Network
   (C) Port   (D) Node

10. Where was the first ever Network setup?
    (A) USA   (B) UK
    (C) India   (D) Germany
11. What was the name of the first network?
    (A) EXTRANET
    (B) ARPANET
    (C) INTRANET
    (D) NET
12. Who set up the first network?
    (A) Department of Defense, United States
    (B) Rupin Balua
    (C) Blaise Pascal
    (D) Roger Benjamin
13. When was the first ever network set up?
    (A) 1960
    (B) 1969
    (C) 1962
    (D) 1966
14. ______ acts a distributor of programs and data to be shared.
    (A) Server
    (B) Software
    (C) CPU
    (D) Mouse
15. A ______ is formed when two or more computers are connected to one another.
    (A) URL
    (B) Network
    (C) Hyperlink
    (D) Website
16. The ______ is a gigantic computer network that connects computers across the world.
    (A) Internet
    (B) World Wide Web
    (C) Intranet
    (D) Website
17. What are the advantages of networking?
    (A) Ease in transfer of data from one computer to another.
    (B) Ease in sharing printers amongst connected computers.
    (C) Easy sharing of Internet among connects computers.
    (D) All of these.
18. What type of network can be found in your school where computers within the computer laboratory and other departments are connected?
    (A) School Area Network
    (B) Local Area Network
    (C) Metropolitan Area Network
    (D) Wide Area Network
19. The networked computers send ______ back and forth amongst them.
    (A) Data or information
    (B) Electricity
    (C) Cables
    (D) None of the above
20. An end system connected to a network is generally called a ______.
    (A) Host
    (B) PC
    (C) Server
    (D) Modem

21. Which of the following statements) is/ are CORRECT about the given device?

   (i) The name of this device is derived from modulator-demodulator.
   (ii) It helps you to connect to the Internet.
   (iii) It allows digital signals from the computer to be converted into a form which can be transmitted on telephone wires or cables.
   (A) Only (i)
   (B) Only (ii) and (iii)
   (C) Only (i) and (ii)
   (D) (i), (ii) and (iii)

22. Ethernet frame consists of ______________.
   (A) MAC address
   (B) IP address
   (C) Both (A) and (B)
   (D) None of these

23. Ethernet in metropolitan area network (MAN) can be used as ______________.
   (A) pure Ethernet
   (B) Ethernet over SDH
   (C) Ethernet over MPLS
   (D) All of these

24. What is the access point (AP) in wireless LAN?
   (A) device that allows wireless devices to connect to a wired network
   (B) wireless devices itself
   (C) Both (A) and (B)
   (D) None of these

25. A wireless network interface controller can work in ______________.
   (A) infrastructure mode
   (B) ad-hoc mode
   (C) Both (A) and (B)
   (D) None of these

Darken Your Choice with HB Pencil

1.	Ⓐ Ⓑ Ⓒ Ⓓ	6.	Ⓐ Ⓑ Ⓒ Ⓓ	11.	Ⓐ Ⓑ Ⓒ Ⓓ	16.	Ⓐ Ⓑ Ⓒ Ⓓ	21.	Ⓐ Ⓑ Ⓒ Ⓓ
2.	Ⓐ Ⓑ Ⓒ Ⓓ	7.	Ⓐ Ⓑ Ⓒ Ⓓ	12.	Ⓐ Ⓑ Ⓒ Ⓓ	17.	Ⓐ Ⓑ Ⓒ Ⓓ	22.	Ⓐ Ⓑ Ⓒ Ⓓ
3.	Ⓐ Ⓑ Ⓒ Ⓓ	8.	Ⓐ Ⓑ Ⓒ Ⓓ	13.	Ⓐ Ⓑ Ⓒ Ⓓ	18.	Ⓐ Ⓑ Ⓒ Ⓓ	23.	Ⓐ Ⓑ Ⓒ Ⓓ
4.	Ⓐ Ⓑ Ⓒ Ⓓ	9.	Ⓐ Ⓑ Ⓒ Ⓓ	14.	Ⓐ Ⓑ Ⓒ Ⓓ	19.	Ⓐ Ⓑ Ⓒ Ⓓ	24.	Ⓐ Ⓑ Ⓒ Ⓓ
5.	Ⓐ Ⓑ Ⓒ Ⓓ	10.	Ⓐ Ⓑ Ⓒ Ⓓ	15.	Ⓐ Ⓑ Ⓒ Ⓓ	20.	Ⓐ Ⓑ Ⓒ Ⓓ	25.	Ⓐ Ⓑ Ⓒ Ⓓ

MS WORD 2010

LEARNING OBJECTIVES

➤ Formatting a Word document
➤ Font Group
➤ Thesaurus

MULTIPLE CHOICE QUESTIONS

1. Given below is the title bar of an MS Word document. It displays the _______ of the active document.

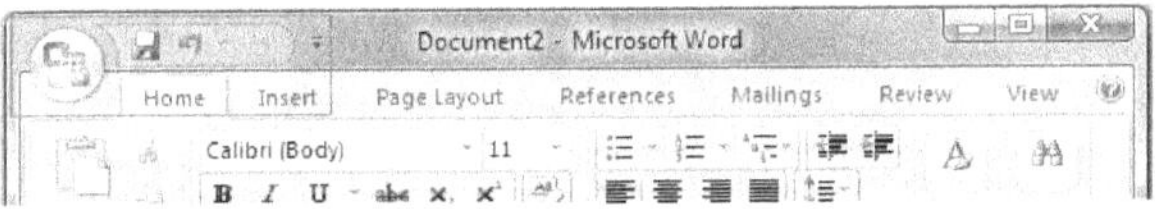

   (A) Area   (B) Color
   (C) Height   (D) Name

Directions (2-4): View the following picture and answer the questions that follow.

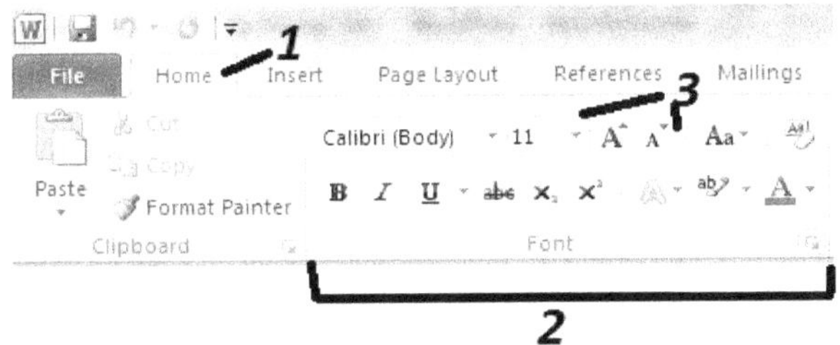

2. The menu system containing tabs and commands is called the _______.
   (A) Menu Bar
   (B) Ribbon
   (C) Command Prompt
   (D) System Bar

3. In the image shown above, Clipboard, Font, Paragraph are names of _______.
   (A) Tabs   (B) Commands
   (C) Groups   (D) Ribbon

4. Match the components of the ribbon listed in Column-II with the corresponding labels in Column-I.

Column-I	Column-II
(i) 1	(A) Command
(ii) 2	(B) Tabs
(iii) 3	(C) Groups

   (A) (i) – (a), (ii) – (c), (iii) – (b)
   (B) (i) – (b), (ii) – (a), (iii) – (c)
   (C) (i) – (b), (ii) – (c), (iii) – (a)
   (D) (i) – (c), (ii) – (b), (iii) – (a)

5. The text styles are displayed in the _______ group of the Home tab.
   (A) Paragraph   (B) Font
   (C) Editing   (D) Styles

6. To view several pages of your document side by side, you should use _______.
   (A) Tools → Options
   (B) Format → Font
   (C) View → Zoom
   (D) View → Print layout

7. Which of the following is NOT a feature of MS Word?

(A) Thesaurus

(B) Britannica

(C) Symbols

(D) Bullets and Numbering

8. The Thesaurus provides a list of _______ for a given word.

(A) Antonyms

(B) Synonyms

(C) Verbs

(D) Both (a) and (b)

9. What is the shortcut key to open Thesaurus?

(A)  Shift + F7

(B) F7

(C) Alt + F7

(D) Ctrl + F7

10. Which of the following options is not found in the File tab?

(A) Print   (B) Close

(C) Edit   (D) New

11. The Page Setup group is used to change the _______.

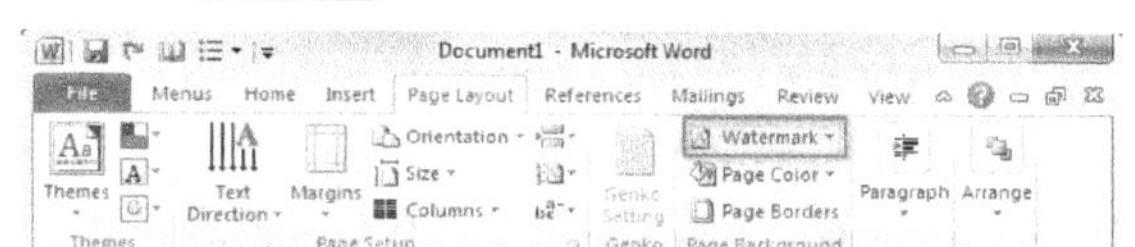

(A) Default margins

(B) Page size

(C) Numbers of columns in a page

(D) All of these

12. What is the shortcut key to replace a word or text in the document?

(A) Ctrl + H

(B) Ctrl + F

(C) Ctrl + K

(D) Ctrl + A

13. Under which group of the Home tab do you find the 'Find' button?

(A) Font

(B) Paragraph

(C) Clipboard

(D) Editing

14. What is the numbering 1, 2, ..., 7 shown in this image?

1. GOLU GOLU GOLU GOLU
2. GOLU GOLU GOLU GOLU GOLU GOLU GOLU GOLU GOLU GOLU
3. GOLU GOLU GOLU GOLU GOLU GOLU GOLU GOLU GOLU GOLU
4. GOLU GOLU GOLU GOLU GOLU GOLU GOLU GOLU GOLU GOLU GO GOLU
5. GOLU GOLU GOLU GOLU GOLU GOLU GOLU GOLU GOLU GOLU GO GOLU
6. GOLU GOLU GOLU GOLU GOLU GOLU GOLU GOLU GOLU GOLU GO GOLU
7. GOLU GOLU GOLU GOLU GOLU GOLU GOLU GOLU GOLU GOLU GO GOLU

(A) They are sentence numbers for each sentence in the file.

(B) They are line numbers shown for each line of the text.

(C) It is numbered text inserted by the author of the above text.

(D) All of these

15. To insert a symbol like ©, which tab should you use?

(A) Home   (B) Insert

(C) Design   (D) Page layout

16. The Header and Footer group is found in which tab of the ribbon?

(A) Home

(B) Layout

(C) Design

(D) Insert

17. How can you format a table?

(A) Change the row height

(B) Change the column width

(C) Apply border and shading

(D) All of these

18. In MS Word Table, which key is used to move to the next cell?

(A) Tab

(B) Function

(C) Space

(D) Enter

19. A horizontal series of cells in a table is called ______.

(A) Horizontal

(B) Column

(C) Row

(D) Cell

20. What is the name of the icon shown by the arrow?

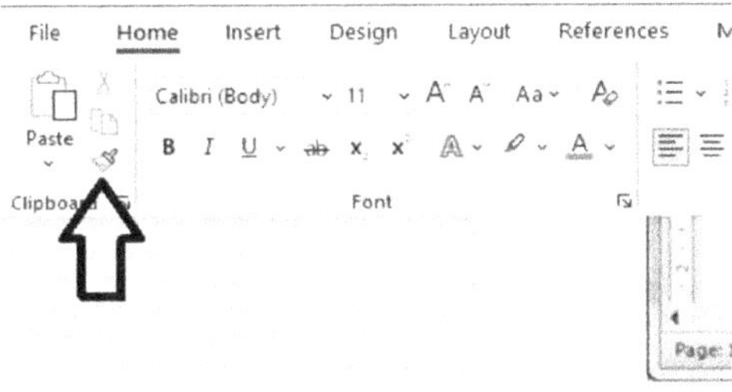

(A) Change background

(B) Highlight text

(C) Format painter

(D) Text color

HOTS (ACHIEVERS SECTION)

21. Which of the following steps is correct if you want to insert these stars and banners in your document in MS Word?

(A) Home tab → Stars group → Shapes

(B) Home tab → Illustrations group → Stars

(C) Insert tab → Illustrations group → Stars

(D) Insert tab → Illustrations group → Shapes

22. Which of the following options is correct regarding the given icon of MS Word?

(A) It colors the background behind the selected text or paragraph.

(B) It comes under paragraph group of Home tab.

(C) You can customize the colors according to your wish.

(D) All of these

23. Match the following file extension:

A	B
1. .doc	i. Text file
2. .txt	ii. PowerPoint
3. .ppt	iii. Word document

(A) 1 - iii; 2 - i; 3 - ii

(B) 1 - ii; 2 - iii; 3 - i

(C) 1 - i; 2 - ii; 3 - iii

(D) 1 - iii; 2 - ii; 3 - i

(E) 1 - ii; 2 - i; 3 - iii

24. Given below are the statements about formatting the text. Select the correct statement.

  i. In MS Word, formatting the text refers to changing the look of the text and applying various styles such as bold, italic, underline, etc.

  ii. After creating a document, you cannot move a single word or a line or a whole paragraph to a new location in the document.

  iii. Making changes and corrections in a document with a word processor is very complex.

  (A) i and ii   (B) i and iii

  (C) ii and iii   (D) Only i

25. Select the correct statements from the given statements.

  i. You create a file only once but you can edit it many times. Editing can be added, rearranged or deleted data or pictures.

  ii. After selecting some text you can do things like changing the size of the font, underlining, bold, delete, etc. altogether and soon. The change which you are doing will affect the whole document/page.

  iii. In MS Word after creating a document, you cannot change the page layout.

  (A) Only i

  (B) i and ii

  (C) i and iii

  (D) All of these

  (E) None of these

Darken Your Choice with HB Pencil

1.	Ⓐ Ⓑ Ⓒ Ⓓ	6.	Ⓐ Ⓑ Ⓒ Ⓓ	11.	Ⓐ Ⓑ Ⓒ Ⓓ	16.	Ⓐ Ⓑ Ⓒ Ⓓ	21.	Ⓐ Ⓑ Ⓒ Ⓓ
2.	Ⓐ Ⓑ Ⓒ Ⓓ	7.	Ⓐ Ⓑ Ⓒ Ⓓ	12.	Ⓐ Ⓑ Ⓒ Ⓓ	17.	Ⓐ Ⓑ Ⓒ Ⓓ	22.	Ⓐ Ⓑ Ⓒ Ⓓ
3.	Ⓐ Ⓑ Ⓒ Ⓓ	8.	Ⓐ Ⓑ Ⓒ Ⓓ	13.	Ⓐ Ⓑ Ⓒ Ⓓ	18.	Ⓐ Ⓑ Ⓒ Ⓓ	23.	Ⓐ Ⓑ Ⓒ Ⓓ
4.	Ⓐ Ⓑ Ⓒ Ⓓ	9.	Ⓐ Ⓑ Ⓒ Ⓓ	14.	Ⓐ Ⓑ Ⓒ Ⓓ	19.	Ⓐ Ⓑ Ⓒ Ⓓ	24.	Ⓐ Ⓑ Ⓒ Ⓓ
5.	Ⓐ Ⓑ Ⓒ Ⓓ	10.	Ⓐ Ⓑ Ⓒ Ⓓ	15.	Ⓐ Ⓑ Ⓒ Ⓓ	20.	Ⓐ Ⓑ Ⓒ Ⓓ	25.	Ⓐ Ⓑ Ⓒ Ⓓ

WINDOWS 10

LEARNING OBJECTIVES

- ➤ Icons
- ➤ Start Menu
- ➤ Virtual Desktops
- ➤ Desktop Background
- ➤ File Explorer

MULTIPLE CHOICE QUESTIONS

1. What is Windows?
   - (A) Database
   - (B) Operating system
   - (C) Programming language
   - (D) Web-Based language

2. Who is the founder of Microsoft?
   - (A) Charles Babbage
   - (B) Bill Gates
   - (C) Dennis Richie
   - (D) Donald Trump

3. What is the full form of GUI?
   - (A) Graphic Utility Interface
   - (B) Graphical User Integration
   - (C) Graphical User Interface
   - (D) Graphical Utility Integration

4. Identity the Icon.

   - (A) Network
   - (B) Computer
   - (C) Recycle bin
   - (D) Mozilla

5. The image displayed here is the image of the _______.

   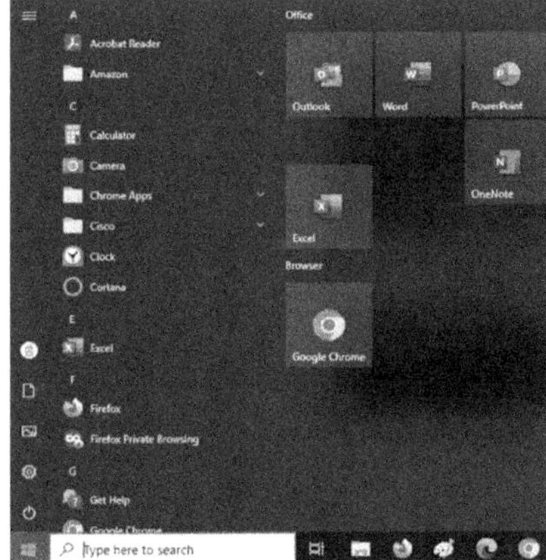

   - (A) Windows explorer
   - (B) Desktop
   - (C) Control panel
   - (D) Start menu

6. ▢▢▢▢▢ represents _______.
   - (A) Desktop
   - (B) Start tab
   - (C) Taskbar
   - (D) Status

7. Which of the following is not present in Control Panel?
   - (A) Programs
   - (B) User accounts

(C) Ease of access center

(D) Windows media player

8. Which of the following modes is not present in 'Shut Down' menu of Start Button?

(A) Hibernate

(B) Sleep

(C) Log in

(D) Lock

9. Identify the icon here.

(A) Action Center

(B) Device Manager

(C) Sound

(D) Ease of Access Center

10. What is the shortcut to close a program?

(A) Alt + F5

(B) Alt + C

(C) Alt + Esc

(D) Alt + F4

11. The visual desktop experience that combines translucent windows, appealing color and graphic effects, and convenient functionality all comes in a group of features called ______.

(A) Windows Aero

(B) Graphical User Interface

(C) Windows Tactile

(D) Windows Experience

12. What will help you to exit a Window?

(A) Open File Menu and click Exit

(B) Click X on the upper right corner of the Window

(C) Press Alt + F4

(D) All of these

13. ________ put information and fun, like news, pictures, games and the phases of the moon, right on your desktop.

(A) Apps

(B) Accessories

(C) Applications

(D) Gadgets

14. To select your desktop's background and themes, you should ________.

(A) Right click on desktop and click Personalize

(B) Type Personalization in the Search Bar of the Start Menu.

(C) Both (A) and (B)

(D) None of these

15. When your desktop is cluttered with open windows, you can use ________ to select a single window and close the rest.

(A) Peek

(B) Shake

(C) Steer

(D) Flip

16. The Windows preview mode displayed in the given image is called ________.

(A) Shake 3D

(B) Clip 3D

(C) Flip 3D

(D) Peek 3D

17. The image here shows a mini-menu of performance tasks for an icon on the taskbar. This menu is called ______.

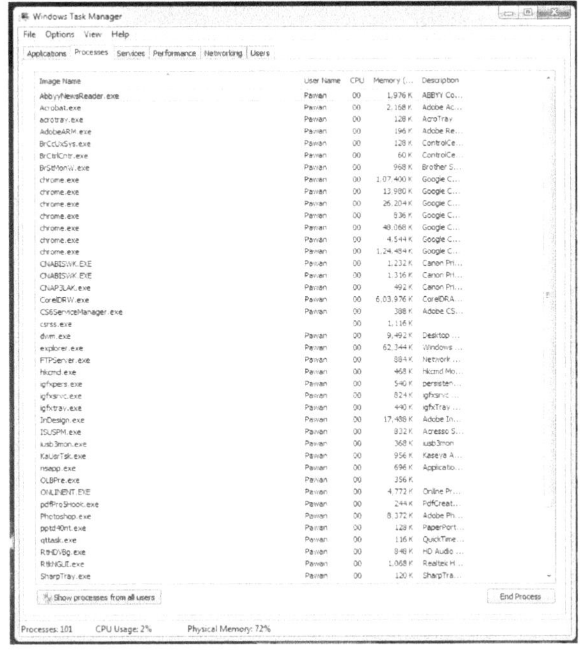

(A) Jump List   (B) Snap
(C) Flip   (D) Peek

18. When you scroll the mouse over the taskbar icons, a thumbnail preview of the open windows will appear as shown below. What is this view called?

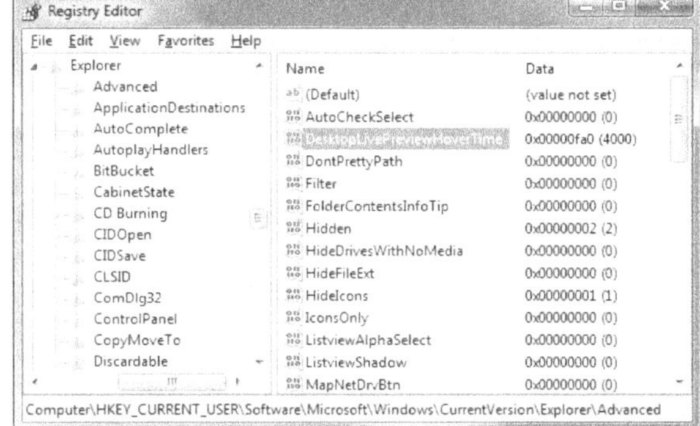

(A) Snap   (B) Peek
(C) Flip   (D) Shake

19. A Jump List on the taskbar does not allow a single access to __________.
(A) Recent files
(B) Remote desktops
(C) Frequently viewed items
(D) Performance tasks

20. What is the basic unit of storage that enables a computer to distinguish one set of information from another?
(A) File   (B) Folder
(C) Data   (D) Library

HOTS (ACHIEVERS SECTION)

21. Match the following.

Column-I	Column-II
(p) Alt + Space bar	(i) Turns full page view on or off
(q) F11	(ii) Opens title bar menu
(r) [Win] + B	(iii) Opens windows Mobility Center
(s) [Win] + X	(iv) Highlights the first item in System Tray

(A) (p)–(ii), (q)–(i), (r)–(iv), (s)–(iii)
(B) (p)–(i), (q)–(iii), (r)–(ii), (s)–(iv)
(C) (p)–(iii), (q)–(ii), (r)–(i), (s)–(iv)
(D) (p)–(iv), (q)–(iii), (r)–(ii), (s)–(i)

22. What is the function of keyboard shortcut - [Win] + [@/2] in windows?
(A) Opens the 2nd position pinned application on the taskbar.
(B) Minimizes all the open windows.
(C) Opens the 2nd position icon on system tray.
(D) Opens the start menu.

23. Which of the following windows helps you to browse in stealth mode?
(A) Incognito mode offered by Google Chrome

(B) Incognito mode offered by Mozilla

(C) Incognito mode offered by Internet Explorer

(D) All of these

24. Which of the following is handy when you take a short nap and resume your work?

(A) Shut Down

(B) Restart

(C) Sleep

(D) Log off

25. Which of the following can give the smallest file name?

(A) Windows

(B) UNIX

(C) Dos

(D) MAC OS

1.	Ⓐ Ⓑ Ⓒ Ⓓ	6.	Ⓐ Ⓑ Ⓒ Ⓓ	11.	Ⓐ Ⓑ Ⓒ Ⓓ	16.	Ⓐ Ⓑ Ⓒ Ⓓ	21.	Ⓐ Ⓑ Ⓒ Ⓓ
2.	Ⓐ Ⓑ Ⓒ Ⓓ	7.	Ⓐ Ⓑ Ⓒ Ⓓ	12.	Ⓐ Ⓑ Ⓒ Ⓓ	17.	Ⓐ Ⓑ Ⓒ Ⓓ	22.	Ⓐ Ⓑ Ⓒ Ⓓ
3.	Ⓐ Ⓑ Ⓒ Ⓓ	8.	Ⓐ Ⓑ Ⓒ Ⓓ	13.	Ⓐ Ⓑ Ⓒ Ⓓ	18.	Ⓐ Ⓑ Ⓒ Ⓓ	23.	Ⓐ Ⓑ Ⓒ Ⓓ
4.	Ⓐ Ⓑ Ⓒ Ⓓ	9.	Ⓐ Ⓑ Ⓒ Ⓓ	14.	Ⓐ Ⓑ Ⓒ Ⓓ	19.	Ⓐ Ⓑ Ⓒ Ⓓ	24.	Ⓐ Ⓑ Ⓒ Ⓓ
5.	Ⓐ Ⓑ Ⓒ Ⓓ	10.	Ⓐ Ⓑ Ⓒ Ⓓ	15.	Ⓐ Ⓑ Ⓒ Ⓓ	20.	Ⓐ Ⓑ Ⓒ Ⓓ	25.	Ⓐ Ⓑ Ⓒ Ⓓ

LATEST DEVELOPMENTS IN 'IT'

➤ Basic concept of Artificial Intelligence, IOT and Big Data

MULTIPLE CHOICE QUESTIONS

1. What are the phablets?
   (A) They are a class of smart phones.
   (B) Their screen sizes range from 5″ to 6.9″.
   (C) They combine the functionality of a tablet and a smart phone.
   (D) All of these

2. What is Bespoke software?
   (A) Old fashioned software
   (B) Multipurpose software
   (C) Custom software
   (D) General purpose software

3. What type of data is sent via SMS?
   (A) E-mail
   (B) Text messages
   (C) Facebook messages
   (D) Twitter updates

4. Which iPad app lets you see yourself in 3D before buying eye wear?
   (A) Glasses.com
   (B) Spectacles.com
   (C) Pulse.com
   (D) Eyewear.com

5. Which of the following is a popular VoIP application?
   (A) Google Chat
   (B) Skype
   (C) iPhone
   (D) Wifi Phone

6. This is a cloud storage and cloud computing service from Apple Inc. launched on October 12, 2011.
   (A) wCloud   (B) iCloud
   (C) Cloud sync   (D) eCloud

7. A word or a symbol prefixed with the symbol # used by services like Tumblr, Google+, etc is called a __________.
   (A) Google tag   (B) Keyword
   (C) Search tag   (D) Hashtag

8. Which of the following is a micro blogging and social networking service?
   (A) Wikipedia
   (B) Mozilla Firefox
   (C) Facebook
   (D) Mobile X

9. Kitkat is _________ version of Android operating system.
   (A) 4.2   (B) 4.4
   (C) 4.2   (D) 4.1

10. Identify the following:
    - It is an app store.
    - It is truly open and social.
    - Billions of free downloads are being served by this app.
    (A) Mobile X   (B) Mobility
    (C) Mobile9   (D) App9

11. Which of these is a Linux-based operating system designed primarily for touchscreen mobile devices such as smartphones and tablet computers?
    (A) Windows mobile
    (B) Symbian OS
    (C) iOS
    (D) Android

12. Which of the following Apple iOS was released on September 18, 2013?
    (A) iOS 8   (B) iOS 7
    (C) iOS 9   (D) iOS 6

13. What is the latest major release of the OS X for Apple INC's desktop and server Operating system for Macintosh computers called?
    (A) OS X Puma
    (B) OS X Snow Leopard
    (C) OS X Mavericks
    (D) OS X Mountain Lion

14. Which of these is a media player and media library application developed by Apple Inc?
    (A) Media Tunes   (B) Siri
    (C) iTunes   (D) Face Time

15. Which of the following apps helps you to share your app's installation directly with your friends?
    (A) Share it app
    (B) Installed share app
    (C) Friends app
    (D) None of these

16. Which of the following is a free video chat service from Google that enables both one-on-one chats and group chats with up to ten people at a time?
    (A) Google+ Nexus
    (B) Google+ Chrome
    (C) Google+ Hangouts
    (D) Google+ Trends

17. What is the name of the Windows 8 tablet produced by Microsoft which was released on October 22, 2013?
    (A) Surface
    (B) Courier
    (C) iPad
    (D) Surface Pro 2

18. The slogan 'Loving it is easy. That's why so many people do' is used to promote __________.
    (A) iPhone 1
    (B) iPhone 4s
    (C) iPhone 5
    (D) iPhone 4

19. Which of the following I/O interfaces was most recently introduced?
    (A) USB
    (B) FireWire
    (C) Thunderbolt
    (D) eSATA

20. What is the name of Google's mobile operating system?
    (A) Window's Mobile
    (B) Chrome
    (C) iOS
    (D) Android

21. Microsoft has announced free windows – Eyes screen reader software that can run on MS-Office 2010, office 2013 and office 365 subscription. What does this software actually do?
    (A) It can be used to verbalize or speak everything on the screen aloud including text, menu, control buttons and other commands.
    (B) It can be used to customize video output.
    (C) It can be used to scan everything on the screen with a blink of an eye.
    (D) All of these

22. Which of the following Indian companies are front runners in cloud adoption and are deriving business value from cloud?
    (A) Wipro
    (B) Narayana Hrudayalaya
    (C) Maharashtra Government
    (D) All of these

23. Identify the following:
    ■ It is an American software company that provides cloud and virtualization software and services.
    ■ It has announced to team up with Google to modernize desktops for the mobile cloud Era by providing business with secure, cloud access to windows applications, data and desktops on Google.
    (A) V Mware   (B) Hexaware
    (C) TMware   (D) Wcloud

24. Which tool is used for image processing?
    (A) MATLAB   (B) IDLE
    (C) PyCharm   (D) SCIKIT

25. The process of finding how many positive and negative reviews are given for a product is known as?
    (A) Sentiment Analysis
    (B) Review Analysis
    (C) Factual Analysis
    (D) Emotion Analysis

Darken Your Choice with HB Pencil

	A B C D		A B C D		A B C D		A B C D		A B C D
1.	Ⓐ Ⓑ Ⓒ Ⓓ	6.	Ⓐ Ⓑ Ⓒ Ⓓ	11.	Ⓐ Ⓑ Ⓒ Ⓓ	16.	Ⓐ Ⓑ Ⓒ Ⓓ	21.	Ⓐ Ⓑ Ⓒ Ⓓ
2.	Ⓐ Ⓑ Ⓒ Ⓓ	7.	Ⓐ Ⓑ Ⓒ Ⓓ	12.	Ⓐ Ⓑ Ⓒ Ⓓ	17.	Ⓐ Ⓑ Ⓒ Ⓓ	22.	Ⓐ Ⓑ Ⓒ Ⓓ
3.	Ⓐ Ⓑ Ⓒ Ⓓ	8.	Ⓐ Ⓑ Ⓒ Ⓓ	13.	Ⓐ Ⓑ Ⓒ Ⓓ	18.	Ⓐ Ⓑ Ⓒ Ⓓ	23.	Ⓐ Ⓑ Ⓒ Ⓓ
4.	Ⓐ Ⓑ Ⓒ Ⓓ	9.	Ⓐ Ⓑ Ⓒ Ⓓ	14.	Ⓐ Ⓑ Ⓒ Ⓓ	19.	Ⓐ Ⓑ Ⓒ Ⓓ	24.	Ⓐ Ⓑ Ⓒ Ⓓ
5.	Ⓐ Ⓑ Ⓒ Ⓓ	10.	Ⓐ Ⓑ Ⓒ Ⓓ	15.	Ⓐ Ⓑ Ⓒ Ⓓ	20.	Ⓐ Ⓑ Ⓒ Ⓓ	25.	Ⓐ Ⓑ Ⓒ Ⓓ

LOGICAL REASONING 

LEARNING OBJECTIVES

➤ Finding the missing number in a series
➤ Finding the missing part in a figure

MULTIPLE CHOICE QUESTIONS

1. Find the odd one out.
   (A) DE   (B) GH
   (C) LM   (D) ON

2. Find the odd one out.
   (A) BDC   (B) EGF
   (C) HIJ   (D) NPO

3. Find the odd one out.
   (A) RQ   (B) NM
   (C) JI   (D) PQ

4. Sword is related to Slaughter in the same way as Scalpel is related to
   (A) Murder   (B) Stab
   (C) Surgery   (D) Chopping

5. Life is related to Autobiography in the same way as Witness is related to
   (A) Papers
   (B) Truth
   (C) Documents
   (D) Acceptance

6. Chef is related to Restaurant in the same way as Druggist is related to
   (A) Medicine
   (B) Pharmacy
   (C) Store
   (D) Chemist

Directions for questions 11 to 15: If MEGHA is coded as NFHIB and PEARL is coded as QFBSM, then

7. Identify the code for VIHANG.
   (A) WJIBOI
   (B) WJIOBH
   (C) WIJBHO
   (D) WJIBOH

8. Identify the code for BHOOMI.
   (A) CIPQNI
   (B) CINPPJ
   (C) CIPPNJ
   (D) ICPPNJ

9. Identify the code for PRABHA.
   (A) QSBCIB
   (B) QSBCBI
   (C) QQBCIB
   (D) QSBCCI

10. Which letter is exactly between R and V?
    (A) S
    (B) U
    (C) T
    (D) I

11. Which letter is exactly in the middle of the English alphabet?

(A) M

(B) N

(C) L

(D) No letter

12. Raju is sixth from the left end and Viru is tenth from the right end in a row of boys. If there are eight boys between Raju and Viru, how many boys are there in the row?

(A) 24

(B) 26

(C) 23

(D) 25

13. A river flows west to east and on the way turns left and goes in a semi-circle around a hillock, and then turns left at right angles. In which direction is the river finally flowing?

(A) West

(B) East

(C) North

(D) South

14. I am facing south. I turn right and walk 20 m. Then I turn right again and walk 10 m. Then I turn left and walk 10 m and then turning right walk 20 m. Then I turn right again and walk 60 m. In which direction am I from the starting point?

(A) North

(B) North-West

(C) East

(D) North-East

15. A rat runs 20 ft towards the East and turns right, runs 10 ft and turns right, runs 9 ft and again turns left, runs 5 ft and then turns left, runs 12 ft and finally turns left and runs 6 ft. Now, in which direction is the rat facing?

(A) East

(B) West

(C) North

(D) South

Direction: In each of the following questions you are given a combination of letters and/or numbers followed by four alternatives (1), (2), (3) and (4). Choose the alternative which closely resembles the mirror image of the given combination.

16. 247596

(1) 695742   (2) 695742 (mirrored)

(3) 695742 (mirrored)   (4) 247596 (mirrored)

(A) 1

(B) 2

(C) 3

(D) 4

17. BR4AQ16HI

(1) IH61QA4RB (mirrored)   (2) IH61QA4RB (mirrored)

(3) IH61QA4RB (mirrored)   (4) IH91QA4RB (mirrored)

(A) 1

(B) 2

(C) 3

(D) 4

18. GEOGRAPHY

(1) YHPARGOEG (mirrored)   (2) YHPARGOEG

(3) YHPARGOEG (mirrored)   (4) YHPARGOEG (mirrored)

(A) 1

(B) 2

(C) 3

(D) 4

19. Which shape has with four equal sides?

(A) Rectangle

(B) Square

(C) Triangle

(D) Heptagon

20. Which shape has three sides?

(A) Rectangle

(B) Square

(C) Triangle

(D) Heptagon

21. Which shape has four sides with only two opposite sides equal?

(A) Rectangle   (B) Square

(C) Triangle   (D) Heptagon

22. Aditya spent 25 minutes on his homework last night. He started it at 5:50 pm. At what time did he finish his homework?

(A) 5:15

(B) 6:15

(C) 5:10

(D) 6:10

23. The cricket match started at 8:00 pm. Each half was 45 minutes. At what time did the first half end?

(A) 8:45 pm

(B) 9:30 pm

(C) 8:35 pm

(D) 9:05 pm

24. The school holiday starts in three weeks. School is open 5 days a week. How many school days are left until the holiday?

(A) 25 days

(B) 21 days

(C) 15 days

(D) 20 days

25. It takes 12 minutes to bathe a dog. How long would it take to bathe 10 dogs?
(A) 100 minutes
(B) 3 Hrs
(C) 60 minutes
(D) 120 minutes

1.	Ⓐ Ⓑ Ⓒ Ⓓ	6.	Ⓐ Ⓑ Ⓒ Ⓓ	11.	Ⓐ Ⓑ Ⓒ Ⓓ	16.	Ⓐ Ⓑ Ⓒ Ⓓ	21.	Ⓐ Ⓑ Ⓒ Ⓓ
2.	Ⓐ Ⓑ Ⓒ Ⓓ	7.	Ⓐ Ⓑ Ⓒ Ⓓ	12.	Ⓐ Ⓑ Ⓒ Ⓓ	17.	Ⓐ Ⓑ Ⓒ Ⓓ	22.	Ⓐ Ⓑ Ⓒ Ⓓ
3.	Ⓐ Ⓑ Ⓒ Ⓓ	8.	Ⓐ Ⓑ Ⓒ Ⓓ	13.	Ⓐ Ⓑ Ⓒ Ⓓ	18.	Ⓐ Ⓑ Ⓒ Ⓓ	23.	Ⓐ Ⓑ Ⓒ Ⓓ
4.	Ⓐ Ⓑ Ⓒ Ⓓ	9.	Ⓐ Ⓑ Ⓒ Ⓓ	14.	Ⓐ Ⓑ Ⓒ Ⓓ	19.	Ⓐ Ⓑ Ⓒ Ⓓ	24.	Ⓐ Ⓑ Ⓒ Ⓓ
5.	Ⓐ Ⓑ Ⓒ Ⓓ	10.	Ⓐ Ⓑ Ⓒ Ⓓ	15.	Ⓐ Ⓑ Ⓒ Ⓓ	20.	Ⓐ Ⓑ Ⓒ Ⓓ	25.	Ⓐ Ⓑ Ⓒ Ⓓ

OLYMPIAD WORKBOOK (NCO) CLASS— 4

MODEL TEST PAPER

Mental Ability

1. From the digits 2, 5, 8, 7 and 3, form the smallest 5 digit even number and the greatest 5 digit odd number. The difference between the numbers is __________.
   (A) 23578   (B) 63945
   (C) 63954   (D) 87523

2. On adding 254 to the remainder when 542 is divided by 6 gives A. What is A?
   (A) 252   (B) 2
   (C) 256   (D) 260

3. What fraction of the square is shaded?

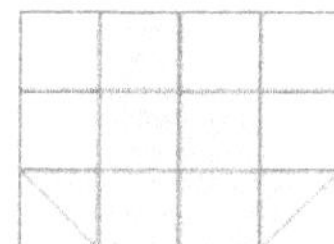

   (A) 1/4   (B) 1/2
   (C) 2/3   (D) 7/12

4. How many numbers between 10 and 30 are multiples of either 5 or 3 including 10 and 30?
   (A) 12   (B) 13
   (C) 15   (D) 10

5. Mona wakes up at 6:15 am. She takes 25 minutes to take bath, 15 minutes to eat breakfast and 20 minutes to walk to school. At what time will she reach school?
   (A) 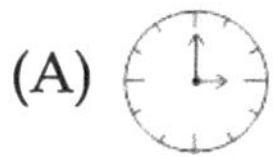   (B)
   (C)   (D)

6. Which of the following is not correctly matched?
   (A) 50 → L   (B) 500 → D
   (C) 1000 → DLD   (D) 100 → C

7. Harsh collected 124 stamps and Harry collected 47 stamps. How many stamps must Harsh give to Harry so that Harry has half of what Harsh has now?
   (A) 8   (B) 10
   (C) 12   (D) 15

8. Normal body temperature is 37°C. When Rita was ill, her temperature rose by 2°C. What was her temperature when she was ill?
   (A) 39°C   (B) 40°C
   (C) 42°C   (D) 45°C

9. What is the weight of one cone?

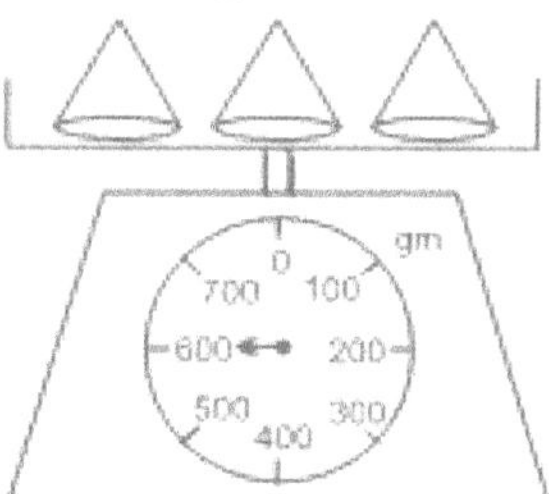

   (A) 220 gm   (B) 250 gm
   (C) 350 gm   (D) 200 gm

10. Mr. Mohit bought 1300 apples. He threw away 52 rotten apples. He then put the remaining apples equally into 8 boxes. How many apples did he put into each box?

(A) 150   (B) 156

(C) 162   (D) 165

11. Lipika gave the cashier a 1000 rupee note for one toy car and two toy motorcycles. How much change did she receive from the cashier?

(A) ₹ 300   (B) ₹ 500

(C) ₹ 400   (D) ₹ 450

12. Look at these blocks.

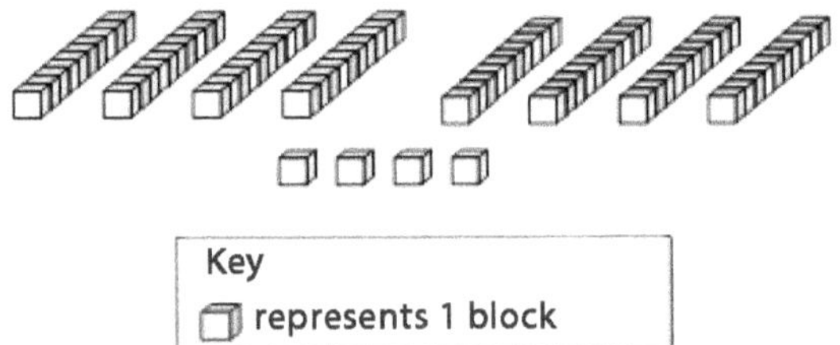

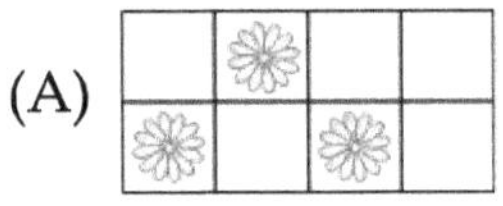

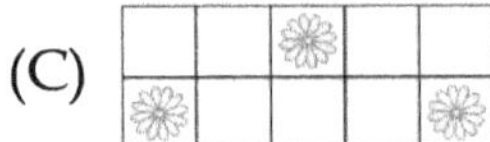

Key

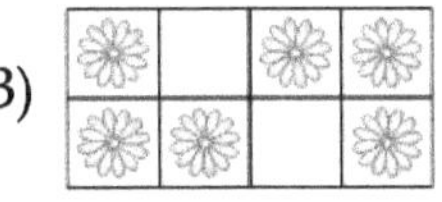 represents 1 block

What number do the blocks represent?

(A) 28   (B) 84

(C) 80   (D) 40

13. In which design do 3/5 of the tiles have pictures of flowers?

(A)   (B)

(C)   (D)

14. Kirti, Misha, Sasha and Annie sold some of their cards at a yard sale. According to the chart, who sold the most cards?

Child	Cards before sale	Cards after sale
Kirti	430	181
Misha	789	671
Sasha	931	688
Annie	842	579

(A) Kirti

(B) Misha

(C) Sasha

(D) Annie

15. What do these figures have in common?

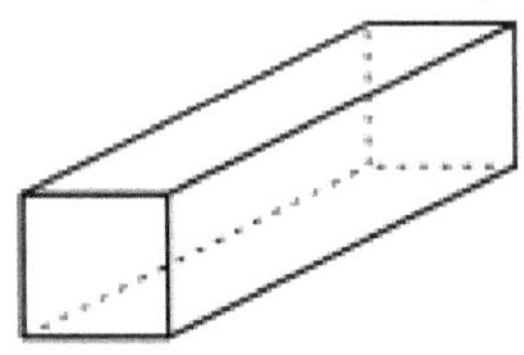

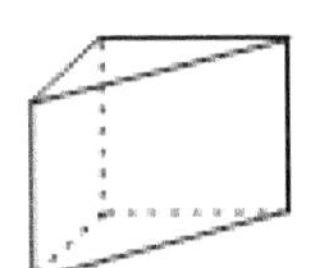

(A) Both have at least one triangular face.

(B) Both have at least one rectangular face.

(C) Both have six faces.

(D) Both have eight vertices.

Logical and Analytical Reasoning

16. Jian made a pattern of numbers with cards.

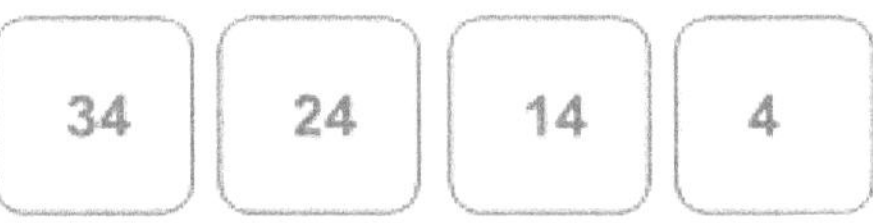

Which rule describes the pattern of numbers on the cards?

(A) Subtract 10

(B) Subtract 14

(C) Multiply by 2

(D) Multiply by 4

17. If $\square + \square = \bigcirc$, $\bigcirc + \triangle = 5$ and $\triangle + \triangle = 6$, then $\square = ?$

(A) 1

(B) 0

(C) 2

(D) 3

18. The given figure is made up of 4 squares.

How many rectangles of all sizes are there in the figure?

(A) 6   (B) 3

(C) 5   (D) 4

19. If yesterday was Saturday, what day of the week will it be 7 days from today?
   (A) Saturday
   (B) Sunday
   (C) Monday
   (D) Tuesday

20. Find the missing number.

123 | 861 | 7 | 357 | 51 | 459 | 9 | ? | 102

   (A) 93
   (B) 111
   (C) 918
   (D) 981

21. What are the next three numbers in this pattern?

| 1,878 | 1,882 | 1,886 | 1,890 | 1,894 |

   (A)  1,898 | 1,802 | 1,806
   (B)  1,898 | 1,902 | 1,906
   (C) 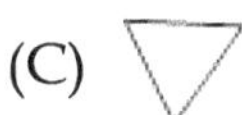 1,900 | 1,902 | 1,904
   (D)  1,900 | 1,908 | 1,918

22. Which figure will complete the given figure to make a triangle?

   (A)   (B)
   (C)   (D)

23. What is the mirror image of ?

Mirror

   (A)
   (B)
   (C)

24. In which figure is embedded?

   (A) 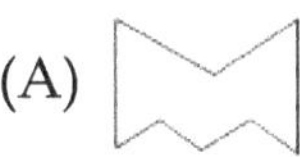
   (B) 
   (C) 
   (D) 

25. Count the number of triangles in the given figure.

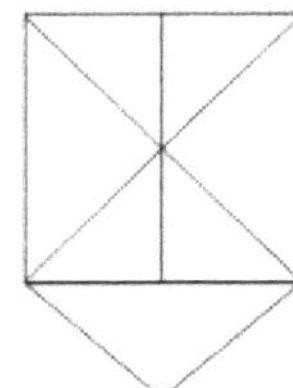

   (A) 12
   (B) 13
   (C) 11
   (D) 14

26. Aki made a pattern by putting beads on a string. If the pattern continues in the same way, which bead should be the next?

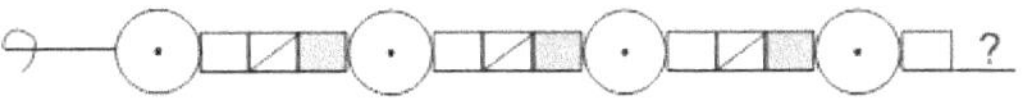

   (A)
   (B)
   (C)
   (D)

27. If in a certain language "RAM" means "MAR" and "GIRL" means "LRIG" then "WATER" will be coded as ______.

(A) REWAT

(B) RETWA

(C) RETAW

(D) TAWRE

28. Ali and John like to eat burgers. John and Aman like to eat chips. Ali and Ansh like to eat ice-cream. If burger and ice-cream are served, which child will be the most delighted?

(A) Ali

(B) John

(C) Aman

(D) Ansh

29. Geetu folded a square piece of paper in half. She then folded the paper in half again. Which of the following cannot be the paper when she unfolds it?

(A) 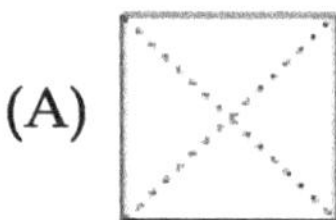

(B) 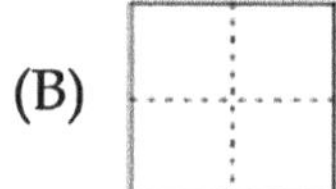

(C) 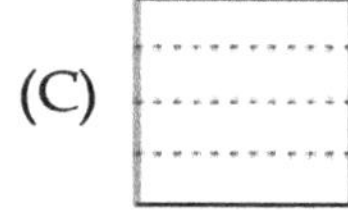

(D) 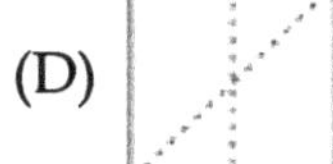

30. The bags shown below contain different kinds of candy bars. Each bag has a different number of candy bars inside.

Nicker Bars	Choco Bars	Sesame Bars	Fruit Bars

3 candy bars	5 candy bars	2 candy bars	4 candy bars

Julie wants to buy 9 candy bars. She can only buy unopened bags of candy. She can buy more than one bag of any type of candy to get her 9 candy bars. Which of the following can be the way in which she can buy candies?

(A) 1 nicker bar bag and 1 choco bar bag

(B) 2 choco bar bag and 2 sesame bar bag

(C) 1 fruit bar bag and 1 choco bar bag

(D) 2 nicker bars bag and 1 fruit bar bag

Computers & Information Technology

31. What general term describes the physical equipment of a computer system, such as its video screen, keyboard and storage devices?

(A) Hardware

(B) Input

(C) Software

(D) Output

32. Creating an MS Word document would accomplish all of the following tasks except which one?

(A) Developing a table of historical events

(B) Calculating the expenditures for the candy sale

(C) Typing a letter to a friend

(D) Writing an essay for history class

33. Which key moves the cursor to the beginning of the next line of text?

(A) Shift

(B) Enter

(C) Tab

(D) Backspace

34. You want to change the appearance of a document from that shown in Figure 1 to that shown in Figure 2.

This document will change in appearance deranging on what is selected in pace setup.	This document will change in appearance depending on what is selected in page setup.
Figure 1	Figure 2

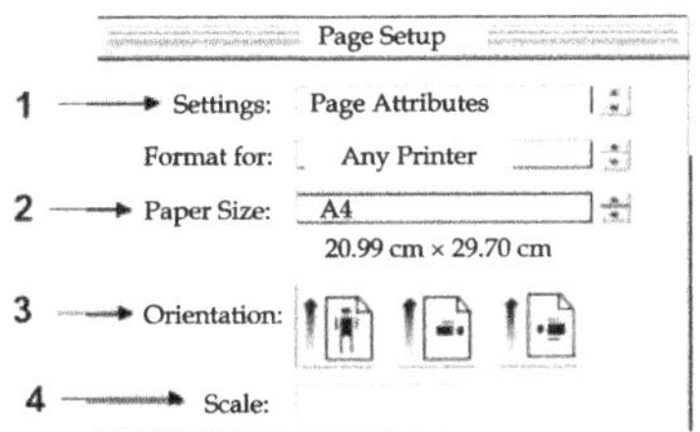

Which area in the Page Setup dialogue box should you select?

(A) 1   (B) 2
(C) 3   (D) 4

35. Yesterday, Komal wrote a story using her word processing program. Today, she wants to print the story. What must she do before she can print the story?

(A) Nothing, just print the story
(B) Check her handwritten copy
(C) Save the story
(D) Retrieve the story

1.	Ⓐ Ⓑ Ⓒ Ⓓ	8.	Ⓐ Ⓑ Ⓒ Ⓓ	15.	Ⓐ Ⓑ Ⓒ Ⓓ	22.	Ⓐ Ⓑ Ⓒ Ⓓ	29.	Ⓐ Ⓑ Ⓒ Ⓓ
2.	Ⓐ Ⓑ Ⓒ Ⓓ	9.	Ⓐ Ⓑ Ⓒ Ⓓ	16.	Ⓐ Ⓑ Ⓒ Ⓓ	23.	Ⓐ Ⓑ Ⓒ Ⓓ	30.	Ⓐ Ⓑ Ⓒ Ⓓ
3.	Ⓐ Ⓑ Ⓒ Ⓓ	10.	Ⓐ Ⓑ Ⓒ Ⓓ	17.	Ⓐ Ⓑ Ⓒ Ⓓ	24.	Ⓐ Ⓑ Ⓒ Ⓓ	31.	Ⓐ Ⓑ Ⓒ Ⓓ
4.	Ⓐ Ⓑ Ⓒ Ⓓ	11.	Ⓐ Ⓑ Ⓒ Ⓓ	18.	Ⓐ Ⓑ Ⓒ Ⓓ	25.	Ⓐ Ⓑ Ⓒ Ⓓ	32.	Ⓐ Ⓑ Ⓒ Ⓓ
5.	Ⓐ Ⓑ Ⓒ Ⓓ	12.	Ⓐ Ⓑ Ⓒ Ⓓ	19.	Ⓐ Ⓑ Ⓒ Ⓓ	26.	Ⓐ Ⓑ Ⓒ Ⓓ	33.	Ⓐ Ⓑ Ⓒ Ⓓ
6.	Ⓐ Ⓑ Ⓒ Ⓓ	13.	Ⓐ Ⓑ Ⓒ Ⓓ	20.	Ⓐ Ⓑ Ⓒ Ⓓ	27.	Ⓐ Ⓑ Ⓒ Ⓓ	34.	Ⓐ Ⓑ Ⓒ Ⓓ
7.	Ⓐ Ⓑ Ⓒ Ⓓ	14.	Ⓐ Ⓑ Ⓒ Ⓓ	21.	Ⓐ Ⓑ Ⓒ Ⓓ	28.	Ⓐ Ⓑ Ⓒ Ⓓ	35.	Ⓐ Ⓑ Ⓒ Ⓓ

MODEL TEST PAPER

1. FUNDAMENTALS OF COMPUTER

Answer Key

1. (C)	2. (C)	3. (C)	4. (D)	5. (A)	6. (A)	7. (D)	8. (D)	9. (D)	10. (A)
11. (B)	12. (D)	13. (B)	14. (A)	15. (D)	16. (B)	17. (B)	18. (D)	19. (A)	20. (B)

HOTS (ACHIEVERS SECTION)

21. (C)	22. (B)	23. (A)	24. (C)	25. (C)

25. (C)
Pixels: are the tiny coloured dots on a TV monitor.

2. EVOLUTION OF COMPUTER

Answer Key

1. (B)	2. (C)	3. (D)	4. (C)	5. (A)	6. (D)	7. (B)	8. (B)	9. (B)	10. (B)
11. (A)	12. (B)	13. (A)	14. (A)	15. (A)	16. (A)	17. (A)	18. (D)	19. (B)	20. (B)

HOTS (ACHIEVERS SECTION)

21. (D)	22. (D)	23. (B)	24. (A)	25. (B)

23. (B)
The Pascaline was designed and built by the French mathematician- philosopher Blaise Pascal between 1642 and 1644. It could do addition and subtraction, with numbers being entered by manipulating its dials..

3. HARDWARE

Answer Key

1. (A)	2. (B)	3. (C)	4. (B)	5. (B)	6. (B)	7. (D)	8. (A)	9. (A)	10. (B)
11. (C)	12. (D)	13. (A)	14. (B)	15. (B)	16. (D)	17. (C)	18. (C)	19. (A)	20. (B)

1. (A)

Computer hardware is the collection of all the parts of the computer that you can physically touch.

4. (B)

A device driver is a program that controls a particular type of device that is attached to your computer. There are device drivers for printers, displays, CD-ROM readers, diskette drives, and so on.

7. (D)

The device shown in the question is of RAM (Random Access Memory).

10. (B)

ROM retains its contents even when the computer is turned off. Personal computers contain ROM that stores critical programs such as the program that boots the computer. In addition, ROMs are used extensively in calculators and peripheral devices.

12. (D)

Today's computers come with the hard disk technology, which is a secondary storage device and in which you can access data in any sequence.

18. (C)

The given device is of motherboard. It is a circuit board that contains the crucial component of microcomputers. It is not an input device and RAM (device shown in point (iii) is embedded on to mother board. So only point (iii) is correct.

HOTS (ACHIEVERS SECTION)

| 21. (D) | 22. (D) | 23. (B) | 24. (B) | 25. (A) |

4. SOFTWARE

Answer Key

| 1. (C) | 2. (B) | 3. (B) | 4. (B) | 5. (A) | 6. (C) | 7. (A) | 8. (A) | 9. (B) | 10. (C) |
| 11. (C) | 12. (C) | 13. (A) | 14. (B) | 15. (B) | 16. (A) | 17. (C) | 18. (C) | 19. (A) | 20. (D) |

HOTS (ACHIEVERS SECTION)

| 21. (C) | 22. (B) | 23. (D) | 24. (A) | 25. (D) |

5. MS PAINT

Answer Key

| 1. (C) | 2. (B) | 3. (B) | 4. (C) | 5. (C) | 6. (C) | 7. (A) | 8. (B) | 9. (A) | 10. (C) |
| 11. (C) | 12. (B) | 13. (D) | 14. (D) | 15. (A) | 16. (D) | 17. (A) | 18. (D) | 19. (A) | 20. (D) |

21. (C)	22. (D)	23. (A)	24. (B)	25. (C)

6. INTERNET AND ITS USES

Answer Key

1. (B)	2. (D)	3. (A)	4. (A)	5. (D)	6. (C)	7. (B)	8. (C)	9. (B)	10. (D)
11. (A)	12. (A)	13. (B)	14. (D)	15. (D)	16. (B)	17. (A)	18. (B)	19. (A)	20. (D)

HOTS (ACHIEVERS SECTION)

21. (A)	22. (B)	23. (A)	24. (B)	25. (A)

7. COMPUTER NETWORK

Answer Key

1. (A)	2. (C)	3. (D)	4. (C)	5. (A)	6. (A)	7. (B)	8. (D)	9. (B)	10. (A)
11. (B)	12. (A)	13. (B)	14. (A)	15. (B)	16. (A)	17. (D)	18. (B)	19. (A)	20. (A)

HOTS (ACHIEVERS SECTION)

21. (D)	22. (A)	23. (D)	24. (A)	25. (C)

8. MS WORD 2010

Answer Key

1. (D)	2. (B)	3. (C)	4. (C)	5. (D)	6. (C)	7. (B)	8. (D)	9. (A)	10. (C)
11. (D)	12. (A)	13. (D)	14. (B)	15. (B)	16. (D)	17. (D)	18. (A)	19. (C)	20. (C)

HOTS (ACHIEVERS SECTION)

21. (D)	22. (D)	23. (A)	24. (D)	25. (A)

9. WINDOWS 10

Answer Key

1. (B)	2. (B)	3. (C)	4. (B)	5. (D)	6. (C)	7. (D)	8. (C)	9. (D)	10. (D)
11. (A)	12. (D)	13. (D)	14. (C)	15. (B)	16. (C)	17. (A)	18. (B)	19. (B)	20. (A)

HOTS (ACHIEVERS SECTION)

| 21. (A) | 22. (A) | 23. (A) | 24. (C) | 25. (C) |

10. LATEST DEVELOPMENTS IN 'IT'

Answer Key

1. (D)	2. (C)	3. (B)	4. (A)	5. (B)	6. (B)	7. (D)	8. (C)	9. (B)	10. (C)
11. (D)	12. (B)	13. (C)	14. (C)	15. (A)	16. (C)	17. (D)	18. (C)	19. (C)	20. (D)

HOTS (ACHIEVERS SECTION)

| 21. (A) | 22. (D) | 23. (A) | 24. (A) | 25. (A) |

11. LOGICAL REASONING

Answer Key

1. (D)	2. (C)	3. (D)	4. (C)	5. (C)	6. (B)	7. (D)	8. (C)	9. (A)	10. (C)
11. (D)	12. (A)	13. (B)	14. (D)	15. (C)	16. (D)	17. (A)	18. (A)	19. (B)	20. (C)
21. (A)	22. (B)	23. (A)	24. (C)	25. (D)					

1. (D)
   $D + 1 = E, G + 1 = H, L + 1 = M$ but $O - 1 = N$

2. (D)
   $R - 1 = Q, N - 1 = M, J - 1 = I$ but $P + 1 = Q$

3. (C)
   Second denotes the purpose for which the first is used.

4. (C)
   Second contains an account of the first.

5. (B)
   Second is the working place of the first.

6. (C)
   R S T U V
   T is exactly between R and V.

7. (D)
   There are 26 letters in the English alphabet. M and N are the two letters in between, but no single letter exists between M and N.

MODEL TEST PAPER

Answer Key

1. (B)	2. (C)	3. (B)	4. (D)	5. (B)	6. (C)	7. (D)	8. (A)	9. (D)	10. (B)
11. (C)	12. (B)	13. (D)	14. (D)	15. (B)	16. (A)	17. (A)	18. (A)	19. (B)	20. (C)
21. (B)	22. (B)	23. (C)	24. (C)	25. (B)	26. (C)	27. (C)	28. (A)	29. (D)	30. (C)
31. (A)	32. (B)	33. (B)	34. (C)	35. (D)					

SAMPLE OMR ANSWER SHEET

1. STUDENT NAME (IN ENGLISH CAPITAL LETTERS ONLY)

Students must write and darken the respective circles completely using HB Pencil only. Othewise their Answer Sheets will not be evaluated.

PERSONAL DETAILS

2. SCHOOL CODE

3. CLASS

4. SECTION

5. ROLL NO.

6. QUESTION PAPER SET

A ○
B ○
C ○
D ○

7. MOBILE NUMBER

8. GENDER

MALE ○

FEMALE ○

9. STREAM
(Only for Class XI and XII Students)

MATHEMATICS ○
BIOLOGY ○
OTHERS ○

MARK YOUR ANSWERS

1.	A B C D	26.	A B C D
2.	A B C D	27.	A B C D
3.	A B C D	28.	A B C D
4.	A B C D	29.	A B C D
5.	A B C D	30.	A B C D
6.	A B C D	31.	A B C D
7.	A B C D	32.	A B C D
8.	A B C D	33.	A B C D
9.	A B C D	34.	A B C D
10.	A B C D	35.	A B C D
11.	A B C D	36.	A B C D
12.	A B C D	37.	A B C D
13.	A B C D	38.	A B C D
14.	A B C D	39.	A B C D
15.	A B C D	40.	A B C D
16.	A B C D	41.	A B C D
17.	A B C D	42.	A B C D
18.	A B C D	43.	A B C D
19.	A B C D	44.	A B C D
20.	A B C D	45.	A B C D
21.	A B C D	46.	A B C D
22.	A B C D	47.	A B C D
23.	A B C D	48.	A B C D
24.	A B C D	49.	A B C D
25.	A B C D	50.	A B C D

Signature of the Student & Date of Examination

Signature of the Invigilator & Date of Examination